AUDREY HEPBURN

A Celebration

AUDREY HEPBURN, COSTUME TEST FOR *QUO VADIS*

AUDREY HEPBURN

A Celebration

SHERIDAN MORLEY

PAVILION

For Graham and Dany with love

First published in Great Britain in 1993 by
PAVILION BOOKS LIMITED
26 Upper Ground, London SE1 9PD
Text copyright © Sheridan Morley 1993

First published in paperback in 1994

The moral right of the author has been asserted.

Designed by Peter Bridgewater

Picture research by Juliet Brightmore

A CIP catalogue record for this book
is available from the British Library.

ISBN 1 85793 267 6

Typeset by Create Publishing Services Ltd, Bath, Avon
Printed and bound in Great Britain by Butler & Tanner Ltd., Frome and London

2 4 6 8 10 9 7 5 3

This book may be ordered by post
direct from the publisher. Please contact
the Marketing Department.
But try your bookshop first.

By the same author:
A TALENT TO AMUSE (the first biography of Noël Coward) • REVIEW COPIES: London
Theatres 1970-74 • MARLENE DIETRICH • OSCAR WILDE • SYBIL THORNDIKE:
A Life in the Theatre • GERTRUDE LAWRENCE: A Bright Particular Star • GLADYS
COOPER • TALES FROM THE HOLLYWOOD RAJ: The British in California •
SHOOTING STARS: London Theatres 1975-83 • KATHARINE HEPBURN • THE
OTHER SIDE OF THE MOON (the first biography of David Niven) • SPREAD A LITTLE
HAPPINESS: The first 100 Years of the British Musical • ELIZABETH TAYLOR
ODD MAN OUT (the first biography of James Mason) • OUR THEATRES IN THE
EIGHTIES: London Theatres 1983-89 • ROBERT MY FATHER
and as editor:
THE NOEL COWARD DIARIES (with Graham Payn) • NOEL COWARD AND HIS
FRIENDS (with Graham Payn & Cole Lesley) • THEATRE 71, 72, 73, 74 • THE
THEATRE ADDICT'S ARCHIVE • THE AUTOBIOGRAPHIES OF NOEL COWARD
PUNCH AT THE THEATRE • THE STEPHEN SONDHEIM SONGBOOK • THE
THEATREGOER'S QUIZ BOOK • BULL'S EYES (the memoirs of Peter Bull) • OUT IN
THE MIDDAY SUN (the paintings of Noël Coward) • THE METHUEN BOOK OF
THEATRICAL SHORT STORIES • THE METHUEN BOOK OF FILM STORIES
for the stage:
NOEL AND GERTIE • SPREAD A LITTLE HAPPINESS • BEFORE THE FRINGE

CONTENTS

Chapter One

THE LAST PRINCESS

"

I decided, very early on, just to accept life

unconditionally; I never expected it to do anything

special for me, yet I seem to have accomplished far

more than I had ever hoped. Most of the time it just

happened to me without my ever seeking it.

"

'I was asked to act when I really couldn't; I was asked to sing *Funny Face* when I couldn't sing, and to dance with Fred Astaire when I couldn't dance, and to do all kinds of things I was neither expecting nor prepared for; all I had to do then was learn how to cope with the results.'

I have, I think, encountered over the last thirty years or so a reasonably representative selection of female royalty at home and abroad; but the only true Princess I ever met was Audrey Hepburn, and she was quite clearly the last in her special line. Her tragically early death in January 1993 at the age of only sixty-three marked in

---

'AUDREY WAS ALWAYS ENTIRELY CERTAIN OF WHO SHE WAS AND HOW SHE WANTED US TO SEE HER' RICHARD AVEDON

essence the death also of the old Hollywood, and I remember now where and when it started to die.

One afternoon in the early autumn of 1963, I was in California staying with my grandmother Gladys Cooper who, at the very end of her twenty-five-year studio career there, happened to be playing Rex Harrison's mother in the movie of *My Fair Lady* – 'because dear,' as she said by way of explanation, 'nobody else is nearly old enough to do it convincingly.'

That musical was the last great gathering of the Hollywood Raj of expatriate British actors who, for more than three decades, had colonized the hills and studios of California to make all those films about the ways in which their own parents and grandparents had colonized India and Africa and Australia. Involved in this valedictory were not only Rex Harrison and Gladys Cooper but also Wilfrid Hyde-White as Pickering, Mona Washbourne as Mrs Pearce, Stanley Holloway as Doolittle and Cecil Beaton as the designer, all working under that most anglophile of American directors, George Cukor.

It was the last day of a long shooting schedule and there, in the middle of a flawlessly and expensively recreated Covent Garden flower market circa 1910 under the baking California sun, stood a cool Audrey Hepburn: the last star of the last great Hollywood movie musical, at the end of an empire and the beginning of the end of an all-too-short career.

Unlike most of those around her, she wasn't British at all: born Edda van Heemstra Hepburn-Ruston in Brussels on 4 May 1929, she had come to London only after the lifting of the Nazi occupation of Holland, which had been her family home. In barely seven years from then, she had already made it to Hollywood for Roman Holiday, which won her a first Oscar; her second, 'for humanitarian services', was presented to her son by Gregory Peck a few weeks after her death.

She was never to live in London again, so her Britain was only ever a matter of those seven post-war years, as she moved from her teens to her twenties; and yet in a curious way she always remained the British Princess. Generations of American filmgoers were convinced that she had been born and brought up in Great Britain. Among the others of that distinctly regal screen generation, Grace Kelly had to marry a prince of Monaco to achieve her royalty, while Elizabeth Taylor, after a brief London childhood, became irredeemably Californian.

Only Hepburn was a true European, and she remained so: she was also, of that trio, the only one to have been stage-trained rather than movie-made. As a result, she had Class: not for nothing was she one of the very few Hollywood star actresses constantly idolized and beloved by such diverse high-stylists as Noël Coward, Cecil Beaton and Truman Capote, all of whose diaries contain extravagant fan-letters to her, written across more than twenty years. Audrey knew instinctively what it meant to be a star, how to keep her distance from the others and from the studios which were the root of her fortune but not of her image.

Like Garbo, she also knew exactly when to give it all up: not for her the slow decline into tacky marriages and even tackier movies that beset Liz Taylor, nor the drug-decay of a Garland or a Monroe, nor the desperate search for an after-life in the twilight of television mini-series.

My Fair Lady was not in fact Hepburn's last film, but in many ways it might as well have been; by the time its shooting ended, that autumn afternoon in 1963, the European settlers had all begun to pack their tents and head back East, their supreme stylishness already overtaken by a new generation of American teenage idols for whom the very word 'Style' connotated at best something vaguely to do with hairdressing. The adults were handing over the movies to the kids, and it was time for the grown-ups to go home.

Hepburn was never the greatest actress in the world, nor even, in terms of pure film, always unique: Jean Simmons had been the original choice for *Roman Holiday*, and Leslie Caron was for a while her rival and equal at the gamine musical roles: both got to dance with Fred Astaire, and it was Caron who got the film of *Gigi* despite the fact that on the Broadway stage Hepburn had been chosen for that role by Colette herself.

But the world-wide sense of sudden loss when Hepburn died had to do with something other than a film career. The last time I had talked to Audrey was a year or so earlier, backstage at the Barbican concert hall where she had gone for Unicef, the United Nations Children's Emergency Fund of which she had become the leading ambassador, to read the *Diary of Anne Frank* to an orchestral setting by Michael Tilson Thomas with the London Symphony Orchestra.

Already heart-breakingly fragile, looking as though she were made of glass, she stood in front of that huge orchestra and gave a performance of such mesmerizing intensity and dramatic energy that afterwards I was not alone in begging her to think about a return to the stage she had left almost forty years earlier. 'It is not,' she said simply and rather sadly in reply, 'that I am a very good actress, you know; it's just that in 1942 my family, too, lived under the German occupation of Amsterdam and I knew so many girls there like Anne – she would have been about my age. That was always why I had to decline to make the movie: I knew I would have cried too much, all the time in fact.'

It was, at the end of the war, the Red Cross and its allied relief agencies which saved the lives of Audrey and her family with food parcels, and so there was a perfect symmetry about the way she would end her life working for Unicef in Somalia, her presence there an object lesson to all other princesses in how best to behave for relief workers, for the press, for cameras, for charity itself.

One of the great tragedies of her early death, and one reason why she will be so acutely missed world-wide, is that while all other real-life princesses always seem on these occasions to be acting for the cameras, Hepburn, the only actress among them, did it for real and with no theatricality at all.

In her private life, she really only achieved lasting happiness towards the end: broken marriages to the actor and director Mel Ferrer and the Italian psychiatrist Andrea Dotti, by each of whom she had a son, were followed by a ten-year relationship with her Dutch compatriot Rob Wolders, who had nursed a somewhat similar Merle Oberon through to the end of her life shortly before he and Audrey met.

Apart from Wolders, what Oberon and Hepburn had in common was a glacial elegance and an ability to cross to and from the world of the high-fashion model. But while Oberon, like Vivien Leigh, could never quite raise the temperature from ice-cool high enough to melt your heart, what Hepburn had was the warming gift of comedy and self-mockery. In the very best of her work, Hepburn alone of the three could make you cry because she had the vulnerability of Wendy Darling as well as the spirit of Peter Pan. She alone was our Huckleberry Friend.

By the time Audrey starred in *My Fair Lady*, her greatest films were all already behind her: Cukor should of course have allowed her to sing it, as she did *Funny Face*, instead of having her unconvincingly dubbed by Marni Nixon, and her performance suffered from the ghostly presence of Julie Andrews (who had originated it on stage) and from the fact that her Eliza always seemed, as Rex Harrison once noted with characteristic waspishness, to have been born in the ballroom rather than the flower-market.

But by then she had given us *Roman Holiday* and *Sabrina Fair* and *Funny Face* and *Charade* and *Breakfast at Tiffany's*, films that will live as long as anyone ever wants to know what Hollywood once meant by stylish comedy. If her dramatic work was somewhat less impressive, there is still *War and Peace* and *The Nun's Story* and an underrated Lillian Hellman tale of schoolmistresses unjustly accused of lesbianism, *The Children's Hour.*

The movies, thank God, will live forever: I first realized that Audrey would not when, in New York at Christmas 1992, I happened to pass a video store on Broadway and see, stacked from floor to ceiling in the window, boxes and boxes of her best films already neatly arranged as some kind of premature memorial tribute, the way that photographs of mortally ill or newly deceased royalty used to be placed in the windows of Viennese pastry shops.

Struck at first by what seemed to me appalling taste, I stayed there staring in the rain through the glass, gradually to realize that this was in fact a wonderful celebration of a great and charismatic career. We shall not see her like again, except of course on these videos: nobody nowadays, in the devalued era of Meryl and Madonna, is ever going to set out to be another Audrey Hepburn. But then again nobody else could ever have been Holly Golightly, or Sabrina Fairchild or the Princess who pulled Gregory Peck's hand from the lion's mouth on her first-ever Roman holiday.

Audrey IN AN EARLY SCHOOL PERFORMANCE

Chapter Two

A CHILD OF THE OCCUPATION

When I was a child, I didn't even comprehend the

meaning of the words 'film star'

'The Holland of my childhood was a million miles away from the world of movie make-believe: I didn't even know that Hollywood existed, and I saw very few movies because I always refused to see those that were Nazi . . . in the oppression of occupation I was left to my own devices, and those devices drew me into the enchanted world of music, far from the anxiety and terror all around me.' Audrey Hepburn was the only child of two divorcees; her mother Ella had come from an aristocratic landowning family directly descended from the royal family of Holland, but was already twice divorced when she met Audrey's father, an

AUDREY AT 15, PERFORMING AN OPERETTA AT SCHOOL IN ARNHEM

UNDER THE GERMAN OCCUPATION IN 1944

A Child Of The Occupation

austere Anglo-Irish banker named John Victor Anthony Hepburn-Ruston. Audrey's mother was a formidable, feisty lady whose two earlier marriages had crumbled because of her refusal to accept the anti-feminist traditions of the early 1920s. Her third husband had also recently been divorced from his first wife when she met him in the Dutch East Indies, and by 1928 they were married and living together in Brussels, where John was now the manager of the local office of the Bank of England.

But this too was to be a stormy, uneasy marriage and it survived only until Audrey was six. Those early years were spent principally in Brussels, where Audrey grew up with her two older half-brothers Alexander and Jan (known as Ian) from her mother's last marriage. But increasingly her father's banking interests drew him back to London, and as relations between her parents grew strained their daughter found herself torn by conflicting interests.

These were geographic, social and above all political: her mother still had strong family ties to the Dutch aristocracy, though very little of their money; her father was by contrast one of life's mystery men, moreover one who formed during these 1930s some distinctly unattractive political convictions. In London he fell in among Oswald Mosley's blackshirts, was photographed at one of their rallies and was eventually blacklisted at his bank for pro-Nazi sympathies. Though Audrey's mother was seen with him at one Mosley domestic gathering, it soon became clear that her sympathies could hardly lie in the same direction, given that her beloved Holland was already all too aware of the dangers to its sovereignty threatened by Hitler's Germany.

This was one more cause for the marriage to founder, and by early 1935 John had simply walked out on his wife, daughter and stepchildren, leaving no forwarding address.

A Child Of The Occupation

However, as the divorce was formalized over the next two years, the question of Audrey's custody came into sharp focus: her father wanted her to remain in England, where she had already begun to go to school, while her mother wanted her to go home to her and her half-brothers who were by now all living with the Baroness's family in Arnhem.

So for the first ten years of her life Audrey commuted across the North Sea, dividing her time between Arnhem and London, where she was enrolled in a ballet school. This was a condition of her parents' divorce, so that her father could stay in touch with her. She was proving to be a natural and talented dancer, if rather less advanced academically, by her tenth birthday in May 1939.

Even the Baroness had become reconciled to the arrangement; Audrey spoke nothing but English, had begun to make friends at school and even to venture out into London, always chaperoned by her teachers, on voyages of discovery to the opera and ballet and theatre.

When war was declared in September, everything changed. Audrey was back with the family in Arnhem and her mother rapidly if perhaps a little eccentrically decided that the real danger to her daughter would lie in England rather than Holland. Accordingly she applied to a local court to have the custody ruling altered so that her daughter could stay with her, and Audrey was at once sent to a local Dutch school where she was faced with having suddenly and rapidly to learn the native language of her mother.

The ballet connection was still strong, and Audrey still thought of herself as a dancer. So did her mother, who was instrumental in organizing a visit to Arnhem by the Sadler's Wells Ballet during her second term; Margot Fonteyn and Robert Helpmann led the company in Frederick Ashton's *Horoscope*, and after the

A Child Of The Occupation

performance the Baroness made an interminable speech following
which little Audrey presented a bouquet to Fonteyn. The length of her
mother's speech was somewhat unnerving for the company, who barely managed to make it back in safety to Britain. For the performance
was on 17 May 1940 and Arnhem was just twelve miles from Germany;
as they danced, German tanks were rolling over the border.

For five long and appalling years, from the time she was
eleven until she was sixteen, Audrey lived under the Nazi occupation
of Arnhem in conditions of terror, poverty and deprivation best captured in the diaries of the Dutch schoolgirl, her contemporary Anne
Frank. Unlike her, Audrey was lucky enough to survive: but as her
mother became more actively involved in the Resistance, and as
Audrey herself took to running messages for them after school, the
manner of her survival was often chancy in the extreme.

Years later, talking to an American journalist, Audrey for
once began to open up some of the worst of her wartime memories:

'Families with babies, little children, being herded into meat
wagons, wooden vans with just a slat at the top, and all those faces
staring out at you. People have fears now which are mostly distant
and unknown: fears of death or cancer or getting killed in a car
smash. I knew the cold clutch of human terror all through my early
teens: I saw it, felt it, heard it and it never goes away. You see it
wasn't just a nightmare: I was there and it all happened.'

Audrey continued to go to school at the Arnhem conservatory
and to study ballet throughout the war: despite increasing hardship,
the daily terrors of occupation, the lack of warmth and very often
also of food, a kind of life went on; and in dancing Audrey found an
escape from reality, the escape that was denied her from Arnhem or
from the very real peril in which she and her family were now living.
A beloved uncle had been taken away by the Nazis early in the

occupation, and other relatives followed as months turned into years.

For some time, her mother ran a dancing academy to raise much-needed money, and Audrey found herself teaching ballet to younger children, even while she was still studying it herself; eventually however the constant lack of real nourishment weakened her to the point where she would regularly faint during classes, and her teachers thought it wiser for her to stop dancing.

In the summer of 1944, returning one afternoon from school, she narrowly escaped a German patrol which was rounding up non-Jewish women and children to work in the Fatherland for an increasingly desperate Nazi high command. Because she dared not risk running home, she dived into a nearby cellar and lived there for almost three weeks, surviving on food she had been carrying at the time; eventually she reached home and a distraught mother who was already convinced that her daughter had been deported. Then, a few weeks later, came the Battle of Arnhem, during which the Baroness and her daughter hid several British airmen from the Gestapo until their own home was bombed to the ground. As the Nazis forced an evacuation of the city which had done so much to help the Allies, they took refuge in a house in the country and lived there, often in a cellar where was to be found the only supply of light and heat, as the last months of the war were fought out bloodily around and above them. Peace came with the German surrender on 5 May 1945, a day after Audrey's sixteenth birthday: 'Freedom,' she recalled later, 'smelt like English cigarettes: I came out of the war thankful to be alive, aware that human relationships matter more than wealth or career or even food. I matured quickly because, at a young age, I was made very aware of suffering and terror.'

Chapter Three

RAMBERT AND REVUE

66

I was the tall, thin, shy girl with the big eyes: but what

they wanted to know was whether I could sing, dance or act,

or did I always just stand there looking in need of a

damn good meal?

99

T he lifting of the German occupation of Arnhem and Holland in 1945 did not mean an immediate improvement in living standards for Audrey or her mother; true, they were reunited with her two half-brothers, who had been transported to Germany for the duration, but Audrey's father had disappeared from their lives at the outset of the war, and the standard of living to which the Baroness and her relatives had previously been accustomed was now nowhere to be found.

An early publicity shot for Ealing Studios

Rambert And Revue

But at least the Germans had gone, and as the last vestiges of Nazi power crumbled, the rebuilding of Arnhem could begin. If Audrey was to continue her ballet and other classes, indeed if the family were to eat, money would have to be found. For the time being the Red Cross was providing emergency rations, more than enough chocolate bars to make Audrey violently sick, and it was then, in watching the dedication of their relief work, that something was born in her. When, forty years later, Unicef approached her with the suggestion that she might like to involve herself in their charity work among African children, Hepburn's mind went back immediately to Arnhem in 1945, to the lives of her relatives and friends that had been saved and restored to strength by the Red Cross, and had no doubt or difficulty in dedicating the rest of her life to a very similar enterprise. The end of her life was in its beginnings, here in Holland in 1945.

The Baroness was as quick as her daughter to adapt to new realities; the fact that she and many of her family had survived the worst of the occupation was triumph enough, and she had little difficulty in overcoming such vestiges as remained of her pre-war pride and position. If money had to be found for her children's education, indeed their post-war survival, then she would take whatever work could be found. Soon after the occupation she found a job as housekeeper to a still-wealthy Amsterdam family who were prepared to offer her and the children board and lodging in a rather more comfortable basement than those they had become accustomed to in Arnhem during the war.

There Audrey, still known as Edda, continued her ballet classes with a redoubtable Russian teacher, Olga Tarassova, whose hugely demanding, intense training soon secured for one of her prize pupils a scholarship to the Rambert School of Ballet in London. However,

Rambert And Revue

before that could be taken up, there was another stroke of professional luck: one morning in early 1947, the Tarassova dance class was visited by a Dutch film director, Charles van der Linden, and his
producer, H. M. Josephson, who were looking for an attractive young
girl to play the minor role of an air hostess in a second-feature comedy
called *Dutch in Seven Lessons*. Their eyes fell on Audrey who, despite
the fact that she had no theatrical training of any kind, already pos-
sessed an elusive strength which film-makers the world over were to
acknowledge in the next ten years. Essentially, as with Garbo, it was
that the camera loved her: her always fragile physique covered a
tremendous spiritual power, the one that had got her through the war,
and it was as if the camera sensed and could even capture that rare
double: the fragile surface and the force within. At any event, by her
eighteenth birthday Audrey Hepburn, still billed as Edda van
Heemstra, had made her movie debut: not that anybody much outside
Holland ever noticed. Her first words in the picture, the first she ever
uttered on the screen, were however characteristic of her screen per-
sona, the one who forever afterwards would be caught by the camera,
backing somewhat hesitantly into the limelight: 'Who,' says Hepburn
in her first close-up, 'me?'

Soon after the filming ended, it was time for her to return to
London for the first time since war had been declared, to take up her
scholarship at the Rambert. Of the chubby child who had left London
in 1939 there was now no trace: Edda had been turned by the five
years of the Arnhem occupation into an altogether different creature –
the emaciated, haunting girl who had decided she should be professionally known as Audrey Hepburn and make her career as a ballet
dancer in London.

By now her half-brothers had decided to seek their post-war
fortunes in the Dutch East Indies, but the Baroness considered that

Rambert And Revue

Audrey was still not old enough to return to London alone, therefore she herself would seek work back in England in order to support them, since the Rambert scholarship covered only tuition.

Mother and daughter found a cheap bedsitter in the elegant environs of South Audley Street, and mother went to work, first in a flower shop and later as the caretaker of a block of service flats nearby, while Audrey made the journey every day by tube to Madame Rambert's famous school in Notting Hill Gate. 'All I ever wanted,' she told her mother at the time, 'has come true: I am to be a ballerina.' She was nineteen, though Madame Rambert had taken her for a mere sixteen and was already worried about her height, which made the finding of suitable dance partners difficult. In later life Hepburn took to describing herself as a 'failed ballerina', although she expressed deep gratitude to Rambert herself for that early training. But the truth had as much to do with finance as height: Hepburn could barely afford to keep going in London as a ballet student without some other kind of income, and early in her Rambert months she took to night-club work, at first humiliatingly employed just to carry a sign across the stage announcing the name of the next act.

What little she earned from this, roughly ten pounds a week, was just about enough when added to the Baroness's caretaking salary to keep them both afloat in South Audley Street, but it soon became clear that the ballet was a luxury Audrey was unlikely to be able to afford for long. She therefore began auditioning for West End musicals as a chorus-girl: the work may have been less classical, but the money was better and her height a positive advantage there.

It did not take long for her to make it into the West End: indeed she got into the front row of the chorus of the very first show she tried out for, the London staging in December 1948 of the Jule

Rambert And Revue

Styne and Sammy Cahn Broadway hit *High Button Shoes*. This had been Phil Silvers's first big stage hit and had also established in New York the career of Nanette Fabray: for London the casting was considerably less starry (Lew Parker and Kay Kimber) though the comic Sid James did turn up in a minor role, and in the chorus alongside Audrey was another long-limbed, elegant but somehow withdrawn and rather dreamy actress also destined to achieve movie stardom: Kay Kendall.

What set them both apart from the other chorus girls of their line was the feeling that they were really only there on a visit: both had more classical ambitions, and in Audrey's case if it was not to be the ballet then it would certainly be the legitimate theatre. As soon as *High Button Shoes* was launched in the West End, guaranteeing her a regular weekly salary of twenty pounds for the next few months, she bade a reluctant farewell to the Ballet Rambert school and went instead to the old stager Felix Aylmer, for private acting lessons: he recognized at once the Peter Pan of her generation and taught her how best to express the urchin, elfin qualities that were her natural stock-in-trade without crossing the border into nauseating sentimentality.

Aylmer taught Audrey a shrewd awareness of the business: before Jean Seberg, before Mia Farrow, she was to symbolize the child-woman but was to do so from a strong dramatic base: being winsome, Aylmer taught her, was never quite going to be enough. She had to be winning, attractive to a much wider constituency than the sugar-daddies she might naturally expect: if she was to be a star, she had to be loved by women as well as by men, and she had to span the generations in her appeal.

But she was off to a good start: she could dance rather better than most, thanks to the ballet training, sing at least adequately

Rambert And Revue

enough to survive in a chorus, and was fast learning how to act as well. All the same, in those days the London theatre was divided up and down Shaftesbury Avenue into strict professional and social classes, and as Audrey had set out to be a chorus girl that was how she was for a while to remain: when *High Button Shoes* folded she went straight into two consecutive Cecil Landau revues, *Sauce Tartare* and *Sauce Piquante*, where she slowly graduated from the chorus line to individual sketches in which she would briefly stooge (usually as 'that girl with the legs') for such comics as Bob Monkhouse, Norman Wisdom and Douglas Byng.

When asked for early memories of Audrey, all recalled her vulnerability; Monkhouse also talked of 'an infectious, impish grin which seemed to go from one earhole to the other and made her incredibly radiant', but what most remembered was her privacy and sense of distance from the showbiz world around her. In later psychological jargon she protected her space, and did not encourage strangers or even colleagues to invade it. From the stalls, however, Milton Shulman (then just starting out as a drama critic) was quick to spot her appeal in revue:

'She had no lines to say, no part to play: but with her infectious grin and her bouncing enthusiasm she actually looked as if she were enjoying herself. Perhaps it was this marked contrast with what the rest of us were feeling that made her as conspicuous as a fresh carnation on a shabby suit.'

AUDITIONING IN LONDON WITH THE DANCER BABS JOHNSTONE FOR THE MUSICAL *HIGH BUTTON SHOES* (DECEMBER 1948); FOUR HUNDRED APPLIED FOR FORTY CHORUS ROLES AND AUDREY WON ONE OF THEM

Rambert And Revue

She also, eventually, allowed one of the cast to break through her barriers: the French singer Marcel le Bon became the first of her suitors to get an acknowledgement in the occasional gossip column, where Audrey herself was now making largely anonymous appearances as 'the freshest face in town'. A number of fashion and society photographers, led by Anthony Beauchamp, had already seen something in the set of her face, the huge eyes and the wide mouth and the look of eternal innocence, which was beginning to get her the occasional morning's work on fashion shoots. Hepburn's love affair with the camera always had as much to do with stills as movies, and it started here, only to be consummated years later by Cecil Beaton on the set of *My Fair Lady*.

So by the very beginning of the 1950s, Audrey was already reasonably well-known around London, if only as a face without a name. Something about her, maybe that sense of being neither English nor American, gave her a useful indefinability. Nobody could quite pigeonhole or categorize her, either visually or theatrically: was she a showgirl, a dancer, a singer, an actress or a model? Audrey herself was at this time unsure, content to pick up whatever work she could as there still wasn't a great deal around.

The affair with Marcel le Bon fizzled out when, at the end of *Sauce Piquante*, Landau decided to save what he could from the wreckage of a short run and move bits of the show into a late-night cabaret at Ciro's: Audrey was kept on for this, but le Bon was fired

WITH AUD JOHANNSEN AND ENID SMEEDEN KEEPING COOL ON THE ROOF OF THE CAMBRIDGE THEATRE DURING THE RUN OF *SAUCE TARTARE* (JUNE 1949)

HER FIRST, ALBEIT FLEETING, BRITISH FILM APPEARANCE: WITH GUY MIDDLETON IN *LAUGHTER IN PARADISE* (1951)

JUST ANOTHER STARLET FROM THE CHARM SCHOOL

WITH A SMILE FOR THE STUDIO PUBLICIST

Rambert And Revue

and returned to Paris. For her however the move was a good one: Ciro's, like the Café de Paris in those days, had an extremely fashionable and influential clientele who came to look at the legs of the showgirls but often stayed to recognize any real or unusual talent.

No longer glimpsed in a chorus at the back of a wide stage, but seen now in close-up amid a company of no more than half a dozen, Hepburn's charms became still more apparent. Nobody was quite sure how best to utilize them, least of all Audrey herself, but in a London still trying to find its theatrical feet after the war there was no doubt that she stood apart from most of her contemporaries: alone and apart, a creature from some other greasepaint universe, with the constantly tantalizing allure of the unattainable and the unrealized. She was also, against all the fashion of the times, remarkably flat-chested: if she was to be a sex symbol, it would have to be for those who liked unconventional symbols.

It was at Ciro's that she first came to the attention of Mario Zampi, then casting a minor comedy at Elstree called *Laughter in Paradise*, built around the old plot of the eccentric millionaire who leaves a fortune to his relatives only on condition that they carry out bizarre tasks specified in his will. Initially Zampi's enthusiasm for his new 'discovery' led to Audrey being tested for one of the star roles, but when she was reckoned to be too inexperienced a movie actress for that, they gave her instead a day's work as a cigarette girl in a night-club, an environment she knew all too well by now.

It was not much of a part, but it did give her a couple of close-ups which were enough to let the studio see in her eyes what fashion photographers had already noticed: the passionate love of the camera, and its recognition that here was someone rather special, regardless of what she actually said or did on screen. For Hepburn, being there was already enough.

Chapter Four

GIGI GOES TO BROADWAY

66

Hepburn is as fresh and frisky as a puppy out of a tub:

she brings a candid innocence and a tomboy intelligence to a

part that might have gone sticky, and her performance comes

like a breath of fresh air in a stifling season.

NEW YORK HERALD TRIBUNE

99

The time-lag between the shooting and the releasing of a movie can be anywhere from three to nine months, so Audrey's cameo role as the cigarette-girl in *Laughter in Paradise* did her no immediate public or critical good; it did however establish her around the studios as a useful face, and she went straight from that to playing the hotel receptionist in *One Wild Oat*, a long-running West End bedroom farce which was being transferred to the screen with

---

THE ROLE WAS NOT THAT BIG, BUT ALREADY THE CAMERA WAS INTERESTED:
LAUGHTER IN PARADISE (1951)

Gigi Goes To Broadway

Robertson Hare (in his original role) and Stanley Holloway. Again the role occupied no more than a few seconds of screen time in two short scenes, and if you blinked you could well have missed her appearance altogether.

But around Ealing Studios, there were those paid not to blink and casting agents were by now beginning to pay attention: true, her acting skills were still very limited, as she was the first to admit later. 'By all the laws of logic,' she recalled, 'I am one movie star who should never have made it. At each stage of my career I lacked the requisite experience, but at least I never pretended I could do it when I couldn't.'

In a curious way her very inexperience worked in her favour: at this time, most British movie studios were already overloaded with girls of her age, contract players who somehow were never going to get much further than minor roles in B comedies, but all of whom were now desperately imitating the peroxide-blonde, arched-eyebrow looks of the Hollywood stars who were now beginning to colonize local screens.

And once again, as was becoming her wont, Hepburn instinctively distanced herself from the herd of hopefuls: she was never going to be 'Britain's answer to Joan Crawford', or 'the English Lana Turner', or indeed the English anything. Vocally and physically she could pass for English, there being now only the faintest traces of her Dutch parentage and upbringing, but somehow she managed always to remain vaguely foreign, a creature from some planet other than West London or the Home Counties, where most

WITH HER FIRST SERIOUS BOYFRIEND: JAMES (LATER LORD) HANSON
AT THE TIME THEY ANNOUNCED THEIR ENGAGEMENT IN 1952

starlets of the day seemed to have been recruited. She was also, unlike them, a natural: not only in the sense that she moved and photographed easily, but also in that (against the fashion of the times) she wore a minimum of make-up and false eyelashes. With Audrey, from the outset, what you saw was what you got.

There was also now a new romantic interest in her life, the first of any real seriousness: he was a young industrialist, Jimmy (later Lord) Hanson, the son of a wealthy Huddersfield road-haulage tycoon, who had already been seen on the town squiring one of the few actresses posing any real threat to Audrey in the gamine stakes, Jean Simmons. Now however he and Hepburn were to become 'an item', even announcing their engagement in *The Times*, before the affair petered out in a welter of conflicting schedules and the apparent disapproval of the Baroness who, convinced by this time that her daughter had movie-star quality, saw an early marriage, even to someone so socially and financially suitable as Hanson, as something of a career impediment. In the meantime there were a couple more minor roles in comedies: first *Young Wives' Tale*, a borrowing from the West End in which she was cast as a shy boarding-house lodger in love with Nigel Patrick, and then the infinitely more distinguished *Lavender Hill Mob*, where she had yet another fleeting appearance as the girl visible for an enchanting moment in the opening sequence.

By now, with these three comedies filmed in quick succession, she had at least come to the attention of one of the trade papers: 'God's gift to publicity men', wrote one of *Picturegoer*'s columnists

ANOTHER BRIEF SCREEN START: WITH NIGEL PATRICK IN
YOUNG WIVES' TALE (1951)

Gigi Goes To Broadway

early in 1950, 'is a heart-shattering young woman with a style of her own, no mean acting ability, and a photogenic capacity for making the newspaper pages among the first-nighters. Her name is Audrey Hepburn, and the fact that some people went night after night to see her in cabaret at Ciro's was a good enough reason for Associated British to talk of signing her for the screen.'

But Hepburn, with her ever-watchful mother in the background, was canny enough to avoid even the offer of a long-term contract at this stage: options were to be kept open at all costs, especially as she could pick up a little pin-money modelling fashion shoots for the glossy monthlies when there was nothing on offer in the way of a film. In this she turned out to be brilliantly right: the list of those who did sign long-term contracts at either Elstree or Pinewood in the very early 1950s makes depressing reading for those who expected such a contract to lead to screen stardom. One or two – Natasha Parry who married Peter Brook, and Honor Blackman of *Avengers* fame – survived well in other media, but the rest of the list is less inspiring: Carol Marsh, Susan Shaw, Joan Dowling, Patricia Plunkett, Jane Hylton, Patricia Dainton, Joan Rice and Hazel Court. If Audrey was to avoid the eventual fate of the starlet, that of consistent professional disappointment and anti-climax, she had to strengthen her power-base as an actress.

Word of her appeal spread through the London office of MGM, and she was even auditioned for the lead in *Quo Vadis*, a role which went in the end to Deborah Kerr who was eight years older than Audrey.

B EING LIT FOR *THE LAVENDER HILL MOB* (1951):

ALEC GUINNESS AT RIGHT

ABOVE: At THE BALLET BAR SHE HAD ALREADY FORSAKEN IN REAL LIFE: *THE SECRET PEOPLE* (1952)

LEFT: HER FIRST SERIOUS ROLE: (1952)

RIGHT: ON LOCATION FOR *MONTE CARLO BABY* (1952)

Gigi Goes To Broadway

The next film role Hepburn did actually get was the first in which she was allowed to display any real acting talent: *The Secret People* was a thriller about an abortive assassination plot, starring Valentina Cortesa and Serge Reggiani, derived from a story by the novelist Joyce Carey. The role for which Audrey successfully tested could have been written expressly for her: she had to play the heroine's sister, who was a dancer with haunting memories of a bomb explosion in which she had seen many bodies. For a survivor of Arnhem who had trained at the Rambert this was typecasting of a rare kind, and unsurprisingly Hepburn managed to give the few people who saw the film (it was neither a critical nor a commercial success) their first glimpse of the star she was so soon to become. Then it was back to another mindless comedy, this one called *Monte Carlo Baby*, featuring Audrey as a film star who misplaces her infant son; it was by no stretch of the imagination either distinguished or intriguing, but there was one thing to be said for it after a cold London winter: the filming was to be on location in Monte Carlo itself.

And it was there that the miracle happened. Forty years later, precise accounts of how it happened are inclined to vary, but this much is known. Staying in the same hotel as Hepburn that summer was the great French writer Colette, who had recently sold her most famous story, *Gigi*, to the Broadway producer Gilbert Miller; he had already commissioned a stage version of it from Anita Loos, author of *Gentlemen Prefer Blondes*. Colette had however cannily retained casting approval over the actress who was first to portray her heroine, for there had as yet been no film or French stage version. Both Miller

THE MOMENT, ON LOCATION, WHEN SHE WAS SPOTTED

BY COLETTE FOR HER *GIGI* (1952)

Gigi Goes To Broadway

and Loos were getting frantic, with a Broadway staging set for the autumn and as yet no luck in finding an actress on either side of the Atlantic with the requisite mix of childlike and *femme fatale* qualities. Much of this was the talk of showbiz circles in London and New York through the spring of 1951, and it seems unlikely that Hepburn herself would have been totally unaware of the search, though in later life she always claimed to be genuinely amazed when, either in the hotel or on the film set (depending on which press reports you read) she was approached by Colette with cries of 'I have found my Gigi.'

Nothing is ever quite that simple, especially in showbusiness, but she did win Colette's approval that season; how far she had actually set out to win it remains debatable. Armed with the old lady's authority, she returned to London to have her agent negotiate with Miller and Loos, neither of whom were certain about the wisdom of entrusting their leading role on Broadway to what Miller described as 'a young actress whom we had never seen on stage, and whose entire theatrical experience consisted of dancing bits in topical revues.' On the other hand, Colette thought Audrey *was* Gigi, whom Colette had after all created. Hepburn was duly signed for a Broadway debut in a role which, by general backstage agreement, would make an overnight star of whoever got to play it.

By now she had begun gently to disentangle herself from the engagement to Hanson, who had made it clear (according to press reports), that he expected a wife to be at home rather than on Broadway, and she was preparing for the forthcoming New York rehearsals when a still more remarkable offer came along. For some

I N REHEARSAL FOR *GIGI* IN NEW YORK WITH ANITA LOOS (WHO WROTE THE BROADWAY VERSION) AND THEIR DIRECTOR RAYMOND ROULEAU

Gigi Goes To Broadway

years now, a script by Dalton Trumbo and Ian McLellan Hunter, written in 1945, had been floating around various Hollywood studios. It concerned a Ruritanian princess on a royal visit who runs off for a romantic adventure with an American journalist before returning heartbroken to her duties, and for a while Frank Capra had thought about making it with Elizabeth Taylor and Cary Grant.

Those plans fell through somehow, and the option on *Roman Holiday* was picked up by William Wyler who wanted it for Gregory Peck, with the hope that Jean Simmons might play the Princess. She was otherwise engaged, however, but Wyler had decided that if the story was to work at all, the Princess had at all costs to be played by a European rather than an American actress, no matter if this meant casting an unknown: Peck in his first major comedy would be a big enough draw to hold the box-office together.

Accordingly, Wyler spent the summer of 1951 in London looking at screen tests and recent local releases, and with all the *Gigi* publicity now around town, it wasn't long before he began to think about Hepburn. Thorold Dickinson, who had directed her in *The Secret People*, her one dramatic role to date, was asked to prepare a test, and negotiations were soon under way with Hollywood and Paramount. Was Audrey, at five foot seven, too tall for Peck? Not in fact. Would she change her last name so as to avoid any confusion with Katharine? No, she would not. Would she be available in the early summer of 1952, after the run of *Gigi* on Broadway but before its nationwide tour? Yes, she would. Could she sign a seven-year contract with the studio? No, but she would give them a two-year, two-picture deal, after which there was the chance of a re-negotiation if either side wished it.

A great deal now depended on *Gigi*: if it worked, Paramount would have a Broadway star; if it flopped, they'd have an unknown

ABOVE: With the great French novelist who was to give her Broadway stardom as Gigi: Colette and Audrey in 1952

BELOW: The film, and the director, that made her a star: with William Wyler on the set of *Roman Holiday* (1953)

Gigi Goes To Broadway

London actress. As if the pressure of the play itself, and of her broken engagement to Hanson, were not enough, Hepburn took a slow sea voyage to New York to calm her nerves, and spent most of it eating. When she arrived at the Gilbert Miller office it was realized with horror that she was several pounds heavier than when she had won the role of the waif-like child. Miller put her on the strictest of diets, but as they moved to Philadelphia for the on the road try out, a still greater problem became apparent. Hepburn simply didn't have the resources to play *Gigi* at first; she herself had always remarked on her lack of any real track record in the legitimate theatre, but what had been waved aside a few months earlier, in the euphoria of Colette's approval, now had to be faced and dealt with in rehearsal before it was too late.

The veteran actress Cathleen Nesbitt, who was playing Gigi's Aunt Alicia in the show, gave her considerable private coaching, and there followed one of those make-or-break production weekends very similar to the one Julie Andrews had to go through with the director Moss Hart when, five years later, he began to doubt that she was ever going to make it as Eliza in *My Fair Lady*. On this earlier occasion, it was the Belgian actor/director Raymond Rouleau who virtually locked Hepburn in the Walnut Tree Theatre, Philadelphia, for forty-eight hours, while he coaxed and coached and bullied and begged and chivvied and nursed a performance out of his young and untried star.

And the crash-course worked: when they opened in Philadelphia early in November 1951, reviews for the play itself were mixed; but for Hepburn they were nothing short of ecstatic, and by the time they reached Broadway three weeks later she could have written them herself:

'A young actress of charm, honesty and talent,' thought the *New York Times*, while Miller, as if endorsing their verdict on his

Gigi Goes To Broadway

star, had the neon sign above the Fulton Theatre realigned after the first night so that Audrey's name appeared above rather than below the title. And there was better to come: the on-again, off-again romance with Hanson was restored for a while, as his family business sent him to work in Canada and he was able to fly down to New York for the occasional weekend; a formal engagement followed, with an announcement in the London *Times* that December, though it was not to survive the increased pressures on Audrey's time and calendar once she started the shooting of *Roman Holiday*.

Although it meant, as per her Paramount contract, the premature closing, in early May of the still-triumphant and sold-out Broadway run of *Gigi*, in all other respects the timing of *Roman Holiday* could hardly have been better. The story of a fairy-tale Princess torn between love and duty, its shooting coincided with the real-life Buckingham Palace saga of Princess Margaret and Group Captain Peter Townsend, which caused a gratifying amount of pre-publicity for the movie. And its director, the legendary Willie Wyler (*Wuthering Heights, The Little Foxes, Mrs Miniver, Best Years of Our Lives*) acknowledged here only one pre-production mistake: 'For economic reasons, I agreed to shoot *Roman Holiday* in black and white, and by the time I'd realized my error it was too late to get enough colour stock over to Italy so we were stuck with it.'

Wyler was to direct Audrey twice more, in the infinitely more serious *Children's Hour* (1962) and then a crime-caper comedy with Peter O'Toole, *How To Steal a Million* (1966). Nobody else seemed to care about the absence of colour: it was a happy picture to make, and opened at Radio City Music Hall in August 1953 to rave reviews. Hepburn won the New York Critics' Award and her first Oscar; it was left to her most faithful director, Wyler himself, to explain what had happened:

The Princess and the American journalist: with Gregory Peck on their *Roman Holiday*

Gigi Goes To Broadway

'After so many drive-in waitresses becoming movie stars there has been this real drought, when along comes class; somebody who actually went to school, can spell, maybe even plays the piano. She may be a wispy, thin little thing, but when you see that girl you know you're really in the presence of something: in that league there's only ever been Garbo, and the other Hepburn, and maybe Bergman: it's a rare quality, but boy, do you know when you've found it.'

For Peck, the memories were of 'a girl who was good at everything except shedding tears: her greatest talent then was as a comedienne and she had done a lot of ballet, been in a couple of London revues and wasn't yet deified by Hollywood. She really was wacky and funny, a very lovable girl who was always making faces and doing backflips and clowning around: but when it came to a poignant scene she couldn't find that within herself, she just couldn't find the right kind of emotion until Wyler, quite out of character, suddenly rounded on her and told her she would never make it as an actress, and that produced just the right emotion and sure enough on the next take the tears started to flow: Wyler had just scared the wits out of her.'

Time devoted their first September cover to Audrey, painted by Boris Chaliapin against a background of Rome's Trevi Fountain: their review began 'amid the rhinestone glitter of *Roman Holiday*'s make-believe, Paramount's new star sparkles and glows with the fire of a finely-cut diamond.' John F. Kennedy declared it his favourite film, and Hepburn's future was secure: never before had *Time* given its cover to the star of a film not yet released, who had never before made a Hollywood movie, and they were never to do so again.

TIME

THE WEEKLY NEWSMAGAZINE

AUDREY HEPBURN
Behind the sparkle of rhinestones, a diamond's glow.

$6.00 A YEAR   (REG. U.S. PAT. OFF.)   VOL. LXII NO. 10

THE COVER OF *TIME*, NEVER BEFORE ACCORDED TO A FIRST-TIME STAR

WHOSE MOVIE WAS YET TO BE RELEASED (1953)

Chapter Five

SABRINA FAIR
AND MEL FERRER

66

Amid the rhinestone glitter of Hollywood make-believe,

Audrey Hepburn sparkles and glows with the fire of a

finely-cut diamond.

99

'I mpertinence, hauteur, sudden repentance, happiness, rebellion and fatigue supplant each other with speed on her mobile, adolescent face' *Time*.

In the nine months that it took to get *Roman Holiday* edited and on general release in America, Hepburn had first of all to return to *Gigi* for a long coast-to-coast tour of America, and then she had time to consider what she would like to do next. In this her freedom to negotiate was limited: in picking up her studio contract from Britain, Paramount had the promise of two movies, of which the first had been *Roman Holiday*. Those few, those influential few, who were already seeing Wyler's rough-cuts in California, or simply picking up word on studio grapevines, already knew that they were dealing with something very special indeed. Hepburn was by no

Sabrina Fair and Mel Ferrer

means the only export to Hollywood from British studios at this time: both Deborah Kerr and Jean Simmons were establishing themselves in California, and they were soon to be joined from France by Leslie Caron, the actress who posed the most direct threat to Audrey.

But something about Hepburn, the model and dancer turned actress, set her apart from the competition: there seemed to be a kind of royalty, not just about the regal Cinderella she was playing in *Roman Holiday*, but about her whole attitude to the movies and the movie industry. Most unlikely to be photographed or discovered sipping a milk shake at the drugstore counter of Schwab's, she was definably foreign but not so specifically foreign as to limit her choice of roles: she could indeed pass for American, and in her next movies she was soon to do so. Yet she remained alone and apart, without the glacial chill that was always to limit Grace Kelly; she combined the elfin-child quality of Peter Pan with, now, a distinct sexiness and a warmth that was lacking in many of her European contemporaries.

Like all great stars, she already seemed to lack an outer skin, so that the camera always caught a vulnerability which made audiences both male and female want to protect her: the truth was of course that her wartime experiences in Holland had also given her an inner strength which was to serve her well when brought up against unsympathetic directors or co-stars.

Not that her next two directors could be so defined; it was rapidly decided by Paramount that Hepburn would go from William Wyler to Billy Wilder for her second Hollywood picture, a romantic comedy called *Sabrina* (and in Britain *Sabrina Fair*) based on an

WITH THE TWO DIRECTOR-PRODUCERS WHO SHAPED HER CAREER (LEFT)
BILLY WILDER OF *SABRINA FAIR* (RIGHT), WILLIAM WYLER OF *ROMAN HOLIDAY*

Sabrina Fair and Mel Ferrer

elegant Broadway and West End stage comedy by Samuel Taylor, writing very much in the tradition of Philip Barry's *Philadelphia Story* that was soon to become *High Society*.

Here, as in *Roman Holiday* (never quarrel with success), Hepburn was required to play the Cinderella figure, in this case a chauffeur's daughter hotly pursued by the two brothers of the family which employed her. The issue of precise nationality was never raised, but John Williams, the English actor long resident in Hollywood, was cast as her chauffeur father, thereby neatly explaining why Hepburn seemed to have a somewhat un-American accent.

The brothers who fight for Sabrina's hand were to be Humphrey Bogart and William Holden, and Wilder was smart enough to cast them against type, so that it was Bogart who played the suave, Wall Street banker in the pinstripe suit and Holden who was the louche younger brother, ostensibly the more romantic of the two but in the last reel the one who loses Audrey to the older, steadier man. Echoes of the fight between Cary Grant and James Stewart for Katharine Hepburn in *Philadelphia Story* would have been even stronger according to the original casting, since Cary Grant was at first slated for the Bogart role. But when he proved to be otherwise engaged, Paramount moved swiftly into production with the Bogart/Hepburn/Holden triangle, so swiftly in fact that Wilder did not have time to get his screenplay completed before shooting commenced.

Bogart, already ancient before his time, was not at his best: he was in the midst of a punishing shooting schedule (that year alone his other movies included *Beat the Devil*, *The Caine Mutiny* and *The Barefoot Contessa*) and was not exactly delighted to find an off-screen romance fast developing between Holden and Hepburn. Nor was he happy about the ending, since nobody had told him whether he or Holden was eventually to get the girl, and when handed a new

Sabrina Fair and Mel Ferrer

scene he asked Wilder only two questions: 'Do you have a young daughter?' and, on receiving an answer in the affirmative, 'Did she write this?' Wilder, asked repeatedly which of the men got the girl, finally snapped, 'Bogart of course: that's why he's getting three hundred thousand dollars for the picture and Holden only half that.'

Hepburn was only on half that again, since her studio contract had been signed before the making of *Roman Holiday*: but here again what she won was the picture. Up against the laconic Holden and the world-weary Bogart, she exuded a youthful innocence, integrity and energy which once again kept the spotlight firmly on her despite the greater camera experience of her co-stars, both of whom proved infinitely more heavy-handed at the comedy.

The affair with Holden lasted little longer than the *Sabrina* shooting: he was a married man, Hepburn did not see herself then or ever as a home-wrecker, and she had only recently decided against marriage to the rather more suitable James Hanson. She was now just twenty-four, and in the enviable if not unique position of having one huge Broadway hit and two Hollywood comedy triumphs already under her belt. By the time the shooting ended on *Sabrina Fair*, *Roman Holiday* had started to open all over America and Europe, and critics were queuing up to give her the best reviews enjoyed by any actress on either side of the Atlantic since the war: the sound of them falling in love with her, man after man across their typewriters, was all but deafening: 'alternately regal and childlike in her profound appreciation of new-found simple pleasures, Hepburn is the discovery of the decade', wrote the *New York Times*'s Bosley Crowther on behalf of all his colleagues.

As soon as the shooting on *Sabrina* was complete, in the August of 1953, Audrey travelled back to London for the West End opening of *Roman Holiday*, and it was there, at a party given by

Sabrina Fair and Mel Ferrer

Cecil Beaton, that she met the man she was soon to marry. Beaton, like all photographers, had taken an early interest in Audrey during her poster-modelling days at the end of the 1940s. In his diary he noted: 'a huge mouth, flat Mongolian features, heavily-painted eyes, a coconut coiffure, long nails without varnish, a wonderfully lithe figure, and a long neck, but perhaps too scraggy.' Soon enough, however, her film stardom made him rethink:

'Her enormous potential cinema success, with attendant salary, seem to have made little impression on this delightful human being. She appears to take her wholesale adulation with a pinch of salt, and gratitude rather than puffed-up pride. Everything is very simple around her: no maid to help her dress or answer the door to guests. In a flash I discovered she is chock-a-block with spritelike charm, and she has a sort of waifish, poignant sympathy. Without any preliminaries, she cuts through to a basic understanding that makes people friends: nothing has to be explained, we like each other. A chord had been struck and I knew that the next time we met we would continue straight from here with no recapitulation of formalities: this was a unique occasion.'

But the greatest favour Beaton – later of course to design the movie of *My Fair Lady* for Hepburn – did her on this initial occasion was to introduce her, at his party, to the thirty-five-year-old American actor and writer-director Mel Ferrer. The son of a wealthy Irish-

---

With WILLIAM HOLDEN ON LOCATION FOR *SABRINA*:
'SHE WAS THE LOVE OF MY LIFE'

And WITH HER OTHER CO-STAR ON THAT CINDERELLA COMEDY, HUMPHREY BOGART:
'YOU'RE REALLY IN THE PRESENCE OF SOMEONE WHEN YOU SEE THAT GIRL'

Why is Your complexion as important as a film star's?

She: *Oh, isn't Audrey Hepburn lovely!*

He: *Darling, to me you're even lovelier!*

THE MAN in your life may enjoy watching film stars on the screen, but it is to you that he looks for real-life romance. In his eyes, you are as attractive as any film star, and your complexion one of the most adorable things about you.

So for *his* sake, care for the beauty of your skin. Cherish it the film star's way—the Lux way.

By making a luxuriant Lux lather and smoothing it lightly into your skin, you can cleanse away dirt and stale make-up completely, leaving your skin clear, soft and lovely to look at, with an aura of delicate perfume.

Audrey Hepburn, whose complexion must always look its best, chooses pure, white Lux Toilet Soap for her beauty treatment. So do 9 out of 10 other film stars. Remember this—and use Lux Toilet Soap. Why not buy the large size—today!

AUDREY HEPBURN, whose elfin loveliness will be seen in mount's forthcoming "FUNNY FACE," says: "Lux Toilet Soap leav skin fresh, clear and lovely."

LUX
TOILET SOAP

9 out of 10 film stars use pure, white LUX TOILET SOA

A LEVER PRODUCT

Sabrina Fair and Mel Ferrer

•

American mother and a Cuban-Spanish father, Ferrer was a former radio producer and writer who had recently made his Hollywood name in a range of work from the swashbuckling *Scaramouche* and *Knights of the Round Table* to the more lyrical and romantic musical *Lili*, in which he had co-starred with Hepburn's only true screen rival still, Leslie Caron.

An intelligent, brooding, moody actor, perhaps too intelligent ever to achieve great Hollywood stardom, Ferrer was always as interested in production as in acting, and no sooner had he fallen in love with Hepburn than he began thinking about what now would best suit her career development. She was still technically under a British studio contract, the one from which she had been 'loaned out' to Paramount for *Roman Holiday* and *Sabrina Fair*, but it was patently clear from the offers that were coming in from British producers (among others, the suggestions that Hepburn might like to star in screen-musical lives of either Gertrude Lawrence or Gracie Fields), that she would be considerably better off in America, where there was already talk of her as a likely Oscar contender for *Roman Holiday*.

And, thought Ferrer as their romance progressed, if not immediately Hollywood, why not a return to the Broadway she had already also taken by storm as *Gigi*? Looking around for another suitably androgynous, waif-like role, it didn't take him long to come up with *Ondine*, the Jean Giraudoux fantasy of the fifteen-year-old changeling, a water sprite who brings destruction to the medieval knight errant who falls in love with her other-worldly beauty. It had been a huge success in Paris just before the outbreak of war in 1939

ONCE A PHOTOGRAPHIC MODEL, ALWAYS A PHOTOGRAPHIC MODEL: AUDREY PUTS HER FACE ABOUT FOR LUX SOAP IN 1956

Sabrina Fair and Mel Ferrer

and was eventually to find its way to London in 1960, with Peter Hall directing, who else, but Leslie Caron in the title role.

The kind of play usually written for British audiences by Sir James Barrie, about a boy-girl figure neither totally alive nor totally dead, *Ondine* was the closest Hepburn was to get to the *Peter Pan* that was always being suggested for her, and it didn't take Ferrer long to get it into Broadway production with himself as the knight errant and the infinitely distinguished Alfred Lunt as their director.

Ondine opened on Broadway on 18 February 1954, after a Boston try out, to reviews that were again ecstatic about Hepburn, if a little more uncertain about Ferrer and the play: 'she gives a pulsing performance that is all grace and enchantment,' thought Brooks Atkinson for the *New York Times*, 'disciplined by the realities of the stage.' The New York *Post* thought that she 'has the body of a Minoan princess and the eyes of a wise old owl,' while the *News* added that 'to look at, *Ondine* is a jewel-box: to listen to, it is rather a trial.' Rehearsals had not been altogether easy, with Lunt and Ferrer fighting for ultimate authority over Hepburn, who was placed in the delicate position of having to mediate between her director and her co-star fiancé, for she and Mel were by now unofficially engaged. Relations between Lunt and Ferrer deteriorated further when Mel began to demand that his part be made larger, and by the Broadway opening they were not speaking at all.

The show itself coasted along on its reviews happily enough however, and within three months of its opening Audrey had pulled off a remarkable double: the Oscar for *Roman Holiday* and the

HER FIRST OSCAR, WON FOR *ROMAN HOLIDAY* BUT RECEIVED ON BROADWAY WHERE SHE WAS THEN PLAYING *ONDINE* IN 1954

Sabrina Fair and Mel Ferrer

Broadway Tony Award for *Ondine* within the same month of the same year, a feat only achieved by an actress on one other occasion – by Shirley Booth, just the year before.

By the end of June, however, Hepburn's health had become precarious, and on doctors' orders she left the show early, to spend the rest of the summer in Switzerland recuperating from what was officially diagnosed as a combination of 'severe emotional exhaustion, weight-loss and anaemia.' By now she was also under considerable emotional pressure, having decided to marry Ferrer against the advice of her still-dominant mother, who felt that a twice-divorced actor almost fifteen years Audrey's senior might prove less than an ideal husband. Moreover Mel already had four children, and a career which seemed at times to go out of focus.

There was, additionally, the problem of her career: three huge hits (*Gigi*, *Roman Holiday* and *Sabrina Fair*) plus one critical triumph (*Ondine*) in less than three years meant that the stakes she had to play for were now vastly higher than when she first left Britain for Broadway: Audrey was no longer even sure which country was her home, let alone where she should be making a living: stage or screen, London or New York or Hollywood? Good to have all the options, but a little unsettling without the back-up of any real career management other than Ferrer's, in which regard it was already being uncharitably whispered that he was intent on furthering his own prospects in tandem with that of his hot young bride.

They were married on 25 September 1954 at a small and private ceremony attended only by their families and one or two local

HER FIRST MARRIAGE, TO THE ACTOR AND DIRECTOR MEL FERRER (SHE WAS HIS THIRD WIFE): 25 SEPTEMBER 1954, AT BURGENSTOCK ON LAKE LUCERNE

Sabrina Fair and Mel Ferrer

reporters in Burgenstock on Lake Lucerne – the Swiss village to which they had retreated from Broadway. Audrey almost immediately became pregnant, thereby stalling at least one of the films Ferrer had lined up for her and severely endangering another. Ever since the Broadway run of *Ondine* earlier in the year, Mel and Audrey had been trying to persuade Hollywood moguls that it might make a good movie, but not even the Oscar-winning success of *Roman Holiday*, nor their desire to keep Audrey working in Hollywood if at all possible, could convince the likes of Darryl Zanuck and Louis B. Mayer that a movie about a sea-nymph falling in love with a wandering knight errant who dies during the Middle Ages was precisely what American movie audiences were then likely to be waiting to see.

If she persisted in the classics, they offered her instead Bernard Shaw's *Saint Joan*, but Hepburn rejected the role and it went in the end to the young and totally untried Jean Seberg. Quite why Audrey turned this one down has never been clear, though the producer Otto Preminger and others were all too ready to blame it on the influence of Ferrer, for whom there was nothing in the picture. But although Audrey was indeed much influenced by her new husband, and temperamentally inclined towards (and in need of) all the advice he could offer, there is no evidence that he was actually wrong on her behalf; saving Audrey from that particular *Saint Joan* might indeed be reckoned, with the wisdom of hindsight, a considerable service.

But Mel already had work to do, a picture in Rome called *La Madre* and then another doomed movie-musical (*Oh Rosalinda*); so Audrey's extreme choosiness about her next project left her unemployed and often alone through that first winter of their marriage. There was talk of *L'Aiglon*, with Hepburn in the old Sarah

Sabrina Fair and Mel Ferrer

Bernhardt role of Napoleon's son, and of a *Jane Eyre* opposite James Mason, neither of which ever happened.

Audrey was after all pregnant, and in no particular hurry to work; the terms of her original Associated-British contract meant that she could be 'loaned out' to Hollywood if ever the right offer came along, but she was under no obligation to film in either country until it did so.

Despite all the care she was now taking in Switzerland with her ever-fragile health, Audrey lost the baby early in the New Year; devastated, she stayed at the Swiss chalet in virtual seclusion while Ferrer hastened back to her during the gaps in his shooting schedules. By early summer, there was a plan to unite them on screen, though this too came in for considerable criticism when once again it was thought that Ferrer was using his wife's stardom to further his own career.

In fact, nothing could have been further from the truth: for several months now the Italian producer Dino de Laurentiis had been planning an epic screen version of *War and Peace*, first filmed in Russia in 1916 but now to be given the full Hollywood-in-exile treatment with a multi-million dollar budget, Henry Fonda as Pierre and Mel Ferrer as the proud Prince Andrei: the search for a Natasha ceased the moment he suggested to the director King Vidor that his wife might be worth considering. As she had said on receiving the Oscar for *Roman Holiday*, 'it's like when somebody gives you something to wear that's too big, and you have to grow into it . . . my one ambition is to be an actress.'

And of that ambition, the film of *War and Peace* would surely be the test.

THE GREAT BALL SCENE IN *WAR AND PEACE* (1956)...

Chapter Six

TOLSTOY'S NATASHA AND FRED'S FUNNY FACE

66

She is beautifully, entrancingly, alive, and when I next come to read War and Peace I shall always see her.

NEW STATESMAN

99

Six million dollars, five thousand guns, six scriptwriters and several tons of artificial snow, not to mention an all-star multi-national cast led by Fonda, Hepburn, Ferrer, Herbert Lom, John Mills, Vittorio Gassman and Anita Ekberg; there could be little doubt that *War and Peace* was to be the epic of 1955. Based all summer in the sweltering heat of Cinecitta in Rome, the film was to be directed by the veteran King Vidor, he who had made *The Big Parade* and *The Crowd* and *Duel in the Sun* amongst fifty or so lesser

...AND REHEARSALS.

Tolstoy's Natasha and Fred's Funny Face

features. But the King was already well into his sixties, and unaccustomed to working outside California: he had indeed called his autobiography *A Tree is a Tree* after the celebrated Hollywood studio maxim ('What the hell, a rock is a rock and a tree is a tree, so shoot it in Griffith Park and save the travel costs.')

Moreover the producer Dino de Laurentiis, fast running over the budget, had brought in Carlo Ponti as co-producer and that proved an explosive Italian marriage; then again, talking of marriage, Henry Fonda was going through a painful divorce and Mel was determined that after her miscarriage Audrey should be as protected as possible during an epic of this scale. All in all, the miracle was that this did not become another *Cleopatra*: in the event it came in roughly on target, and opened to politely respectful reviews around the world.

Those who wanted the true *War and Peace* on screen would however have to wait until 1967 for the Soviet version by Bondarchuk, who was to spend five years and seventy million dollars on the project: this earlier version raised a gentle yawn from audiences around the world but no feeling that the essential Tolstoy had been captured on the wide screen. 'Too much peace, not enough war' was one verdict, while others felt that the attempt to rebuild Moscow on the banks of the Tiber was doomed from the outset by Vidor's determination that this was to be his *Gone With the Wind*. 'Just one little difference,' noted an observer icily, 'where Vivien Leigh was Scarlett O'Hara, here Natasha is Audrey Hepburn.'

Another American critic began to note that 'Audrey Hepburn's appeal, it becomes clearer with every appearance, is largely to the imagination; the less acting she does, the more people can imagine her doing, and wisely she usually does very little on screen, but that little she does with extreme skill.'

Tolstoy's Natasha and Fred's Funny Face

This was to be a recurring theme in critical attitudes to Hepburn: the fact that she had started as a dancer, with virtually no stage training in the classics and only a brief rehearsal period before *Gigi* and then *Ondine* on Broadway, made her success there all the more remarkable, but it also gave her certain doubts about herself as a 'legitimate' stage actress, and after her collapse during the run of *Ondine* she was never again, in a career which spanned the next forty years, to return to the theatre.

Instead, her thoughts were now firmly trained on trying to start a family with Ferrer, who was maintaining a thriving film career on both sides of the Atlantic, despite his rather qualified reviews for *War and Peace*: 'a certain sullen grandeur, but diction often unclear,' thought *Time* magazine, adding 'Henry Fonda is the only one in this huge cast who looks as though he might actually have read the book,' an unfair reflection on Audrey who, with her customary meticulous research, had not only read the original but also several critical studies of Tolstoy and his period along the way.

By the time that the long, hot summer of 1955 came to an end, with *War and Peace* at last in the can at Cinecitta, Hepburn and Ferrer had to consider what, if she was not to become immediately pregnant again, she should play next. One suggestion was Tennessee Williams's *Summer and Smoke*, but after the rigours of *War and Peace* Audrey was inclined to go back to something rather lighter; she had never yet, except in fleeting moments of *Sabrina* and *Roman Holiday*, used any of her old dancing skills, and there were rumours of a new Fred Astaire musical on the horizon. With Ginger

To HER BELOVED PARIS FOR *FUNNY FACE* (1957): DANCING IN THE RAIN FOR HER FRIEND AND CAMERAMAN, RICHARD AVEDON

Tolstoy's Natasha and Fred's Funny Face

Rogers long gone, and no other regular co-star established, might he in fact be in search of a dancing partner?

Astaire was; the film was to be a drastically revised version of the Gershwins' *Funny Face*, in which Fred and his sister Adele had starred on Broadway and in the West End for two years at the very end of the 1920s. Now, with a totally restructured plot loosely based on the life of the film's 'visual consultant', the photographer Richard Avedon who was to become one of Audrey's closest friends and most constant cameramen, *Funny Face* resurfaced amidst a welter of contractual problems.

Briefly, the difficulty was that whereas MGM owned the rights to the script and to the producer Roger Edens, who had worked so triumphantly with Astaire on *Easter Parade* and *The Band Wagon*, Paramount owned the rights to Audrey Hepburn who by general agreement was as near-perfect casting as they would get for the shy, Greenwich Village bookstore worker who gets literally swept off her feet to Paris by Astaire in one of the last great Hollywood musicals.

The shooting, first at Paramount in Hollywood and then on location in Paris itself, was not without its problems: during one sequence, shot after a violent rainstorm, Audrey fell flat on her face: 'all my life I dream of dancing with Astaire and what do I get? Caked in mud.' Astaire's old friend and choreographer Hermes Pan came to watch the shooting, having literally been guided into the arc lights while wandering through the city in search of his hotel. But one or two other observers began to feel that the film was in danger of being stolen from its two stars by the unique and irrepressible cabaret artist Kay Thompson, Liza Minnelli's great mentor, here in a rare screen appearance as the doyenne fashion editor of *Vogue* who, in one of the movie's best production numbers, insists that everyone 'Think Pink'.

Tolstoy's Natasha and Fred's Funny Face

But despite the thirty-year difference in their ages (Astaire was now fifty-seven), there was something very magical in the Fred and Audrey teaming ('Yeah, something old, something new,' muttered one cynic), which was best recalled by Audrey herself in a speech she made twenty years later at Astaire's Life Achievement Award ceremony:

'I remember the first time we met: he was wearing a yellow shirt, grey flannels, a red scarf knotted around his waist instead of a belt, and the famous feet were clad in soft moccasins and pink socks. He was also wearing that irrepressible smile. One look at this most debonair, elegant and distinguished of legends and I could feel myself turn to solid lead, while my heart sank into my two left feet. Then suddenly I felt a hand around my waist and, with his inimitable grace and lightness, Fred literally swept me off my feet. I experienced the thrill that all women at some point in their lives have dreamed of – to dance, just once, with Fred Astaire.'

And not only to dance: in numbers like 'How Long Has This Been Going On?' and 'S'Wonderful', Audrey established an enchanting screen-musical presence, one to which she alas was never to return, and which was to be rashly overlooked by the makers of *My Fair Lady* when they decided that she had to be dubbed. So here, uniquely, is the all-singing all-dancing Audrey Hepburn in a film which once again required Astaire to take a much younger partner (not unlike the Rita Hayworth character in *Cover Girl*, though she was already a model) and transform her, through dance. Astaire photographing Hepburn against all the classic landmarks of Paris became a cinematic metaphor for the way that Audrey herself was

THE LEFT BANK NIGHTCLUB SEQUENCE FROM *FUNNY FACE*

Tolstoy's Natasha and Fred's Funny Face

somehow simultaneously now being released and transfixed by the movie camera, itself able to convey, long before the term became fashionable, an image perhaps more potent than the reality of what she was as an actress.

Her screen innocence was now a matter of fantasy rather than fact: she and Ferrer had been able to drive a hard bargain on the *Funny Face* contract, for which she received seventy-five thousand pounds and a living allowance large enough to retain an entire suite at the Ritz as well as the right to retain much of her Givenchy wardrobe: 'She is the perfect model for me,' said the great French couturier, 'she has an ideal face and figure with that long, slim body and swan-like neck.' From now on, a clause in her film contracts would insist wherever possible on 'clothes by Givenchy'. But it was with *Funny Face* that the whole, elfin, enchanting Hepburn image first came fully into focus. Seen again forty years after it was made, the film stands up superbly against the better-known *An American in Paris*: where Gene Kelly and Leslie Caron have energy, Astaire and Hepburn have class and style and subtlety, and it makes all the difference between a good Parisian musical and a great one. If only Audrey had also managed to make *Gigi* for the screen a couple of years later . . . but by then she was alas otherwise engaged, and her role went by default to Caron.

As the critic Clive Hirschhorn has noted, *Funny Face* was 'a Paramount production with all the panache of a vintage MGM musical, no accident this since both its producer Roger Edens and its director Stanley Donen were members of Arthur Freed's unit at

ON THE *FUNNY FACE* SET WITH THE MAN WHO BECAME HER LIFELONG DESIGNER AND FRIEND, HUBERT DE GIVENCHY

Tolstoy's Natasha and Fred's Funny Face

Culver City . . . the story of the waif-like Greenwich Village book-seller who is discovered by a fashion photographer and whisked off to Paris to be transformed into a top model had its tongue in its cheek in its attitudes to the synthetic milieu of high fashion, and also took a few jibes at the then popular Existential movement . . . though Astaire was getting too old to play the romantic lead, he sub-stituted charm for youth and Avedon's work as visual consultant resulted in *Funny Face* being the most ravishingly photographed musical of its time.'

And for Audrey herself, as she told Sarah Giles soon after Fred's death, the memories were nothing but great: 'Was he romantic? Well, *Funny Face* was a romantic movie . . . he was a very, very dear man . . . did he give me confidence? Oh yes, from the very first minute. Before we actually started rehearsing the num-ber he said, "Come on, let's have a little go together," and we just danced around together. . . . Fred and I didn't spend a lot of time together socially, because on a picture like that one got so bushed and one had to get up early. . . . We went to Paris and it rained a lot, very soggy . . . my clothes were all by Givenchy and they still look pretty good but Fred never asked about them before shooting. he was always very low-key, very relaxed and I was just so lucky to be working with a legend.'

'HE JUST MADE IT ALL SEEM SO EASY': WITH FRED ASTAIRE

ON THE SET OF *FUNNY FACE*

Chapter Seven

LOVE IN THE AFTERNOON AND A NUN IN THE BELGIAN CONGO

66

Hepburn has generally been equal in talent and technique to whatever she has been asked to do; but after she has done all that can be done by knowledge and design, her beauty speaks for her in the remarkable way that it serves as an intensifying glass for whatever inner travail she is trying to convey.

STANLEY KAUFFMAN

99

Mr and mrs ferrer set sail for Europe

Love In The Afternoon And A Nun In The Belgian Congo

F or her next picture, Hepburn was to stay on location in Paris; there she had hoped to be joined by the actor she still most wanted to play opposite, Cary Grant; but Grant was a wily old bird who, unlike Astaire, realized that he had to be very careful about the age gap between him and a new co-star. Soon enough, he would find the perfect vehicle for himself and Audrey, but it was not to be a conventional love story. *Love in the Afternoon* was just that, and the role of the American playboy falling in love with the daughter of his Parisian private detective was thus taken on by an already ailing Gary Cooper. As Grant had suspected, a number of critics declared themselves faintly uneasy about the generation gap when the two had to play quite explicit love scenes. Ironically the actor who might have got away with them was also in the film, Maurice Chevalier, but here he was cast as Audrey's father.

Love in the Afternoon was a Billy Wilder production, but there was something about Parisian locations (as in the later *Irma La Douce* with Shirley MacLaine) which invariably caused Wilder and his co-writer I. A. L. Diamond to lose their sure-fire comic touch, with the result that despite its gorgeous sets and costumes this turned out to be Hepburn's first major failure, not so much at the box-office as among those hitherto devoted critics on both sides of the Atlantic who had no desire to see their golden girl caught up in a somewhat tawdry affair with a movie star well past his prime and certainly old enough to be her father.

The American distributors, in high moral fervour, panicked at

---

A T HOME AND ABROAD WITH MEL

B ACK TO PARIS, FOR LOVE IN THE AFTERNOON (1956): GARY COOPER AS HER LOVER (LEFT), MAURICE CHEVALIER AS HER FATHER (RIGHT)

A COMEDY THAT NEVER MANAGED TO MAKE ITS AUDIENCES FORGET THE FACT
THAT COOP WAS OLD ENOUGH TO BE HIS LOVER'S FATHER

Love In The Afternoon And
A Nun In The Belgian Congo

the early 'bad taste' reactions to the movie in the US, and even went so far as to add a voice-over at the end indicating that the extramarital lovers would in fact soon be heading for the altar. European audiences were deemed more sophisticated and therefore in need of no such reassurance, and indeed one of the constants of Hepburn's career was to be her habit of playing opposite much older leading men, from Gregory Peck through Humphrey Bogart, Henry Fonda, Fred Astaire and Gary Cooper to Rex Harrison and Cary Grant. But here somehow the chemistry was wrong, and Audrey's image, at least in Middle America, suffered its first real damage.

Perhaps because of this, although more possibly because of her increasingly desperate desire to have a child, she then announced early in 1957 that she would be taking at least a year off from filming, thereby neatly avoiding *A Certain Smile* (the Françoise Sagan disaster) but also turning down *The Diary of Anne Frank* (which went eventually to Millie Perkins). Other suggestions for employment included a return to the Broadway stage in the musical of *Zuleika*, Max Beerbohm's tale of the magical maiden driving Oxford undergraduates to their death, which had recently been tried not very successfully on the London stage.

Given her childhood in occupied Holland, *The Diary of Anne Frank* has always of course had a special meaning for Audrey, and she found the Broadway play unbearably moving; for just that reason, she felt she had to avoid the movie: it would bring back too many terrible memories.

Instead, after a few weeks off she turned to television, making one of her very rare appearances there in an early NBC colour dramatization of *Mayerling* for which, under Anatole Litvak's direction, she was to play opposite Mel Ferrer as the doomed lovers of the Habsburg double-suicide plot, a regular standby for moviemakers over the years from Charles Boyer and Danielle Darrieux (1936) to Omar Sharif and

WITH MAURICE CHEVALIER AS HER FATHER

IN *LOVE IN THE AFTERNOON*

Love In The Afternoon And
A Nun In The Belgian Congo

Catherine Deneuve (1968). The Ferrer–Hepburn version was given a very limited cinema release in Europe the following year, but had by then attracted dismal reviews from American television reviewers who reckoned that Ferrer was somewhat ancient already for the lovelorn young Crown Prince: 'The lovers seemed more fated to bore each other to death than to die in a murder-suicide pact' commented one, while not even the casting of Raymond Massey and Diana Wynyard as the imperial parents could retrieve this.

By now it was beginning to dawn, certainly on Audrey and more grudgingly on Mel, that they were not destined to be the next Laurence Olivier and Vivien Leigh: a public which would accept Hepburn as a radiant leading lady and Ferrer as a useful if downbeat character actor was not prepared to take them as a romantic double, and from now on Ferrer began to think of himself as the producer/director rather than co-star of the partnership.

That still left open the question of what Audrey should play next, and here an uneasy truth began to emerge: although she was already fashion's darling, beloved of photographers and designers and magazine editors on both sides of the Atlantic, Audrey was not all that easy to cast in actual movies. As she emerged from gamine, understandably determined not to be forever typecast as a kind of asexual Peter Pan, so too Hollywood was emerging from its thirty-year affair with elegance and charm and discretion, and moving towards a grainy new 1950s realism in which this Hepburn seemed almost as much of a misfit as her older namesake.

In Californian terms, Audrey was as palpably foreign as Juliette Greco: a child of post-war Europe, she was already making her influence felt on glossy fashion pages but not necessarily around the offices of casting directors. It was, at this time, one of her first and best chroniclers, Cecil Beaton, who perceived the problem:

Love In The Afternoon And A Nun In The Belgian Congo

'Her facial features show character rather than prettiness: the bridge of the nose seems almost too narrow to carry its length, which flares into nostrils startlingly like a duck's bill . . . her mouth is wide, with a cleft under the lower lip too deep for classical beauty, and the delicate chin appears even smaller by contrast with the exaggerated width of her jawbone; seen at the full, the outline of her face is perhaps too square, yet she intuitively tilts her head with a restless and perky asymmetry . . . a combination of fashion plate and ballet dancer.

'Audrey Hepburn is the gamine, the urchin, the lost Barnardo Boy: sometimes, already, she seems dangerously fatigued, the wistful child of a war-torn era, and the shadow that was thrown across her youth in Holland underlines even more its precious evanescence. It is rare to find a young girl with such inherent and immediate star quality, and as a result of her enormous success she had already acquired the extra, incandescent glow which comes as a result of being acclaimed, admired and loved. Yet while developing her radiance, she has too much innate candour to take on the gloss of artificiality that Hollywood is apt to demand of its queens. Her voice is peculiarly personal, with its unaccustomed rhythm and sing-song cadences; it has the quality of heartbreak.'

And for that 'quality of heartbreak', what better to try next than a bestseller about a nun losing her faith in the Belgian Congo? Kathryn C. Hulme's novel had been on the Hollywood agenda for several months now, but without much immediate enthusiasm: a semi-documentary about a nun was not reckoned likely to enter high on the box-office

---

WITH FRED ZINNEMANN, DIRECTOR OF *THE NUN'S STORY* (1959) WHICH WON HER A THIRD OSCAR NOMINATION AND THE NEW YORK CRITICS' AWARD

WITH PETER FINCH AS THE DOCTOR WHO THREATENS HER NUN'S VOWS

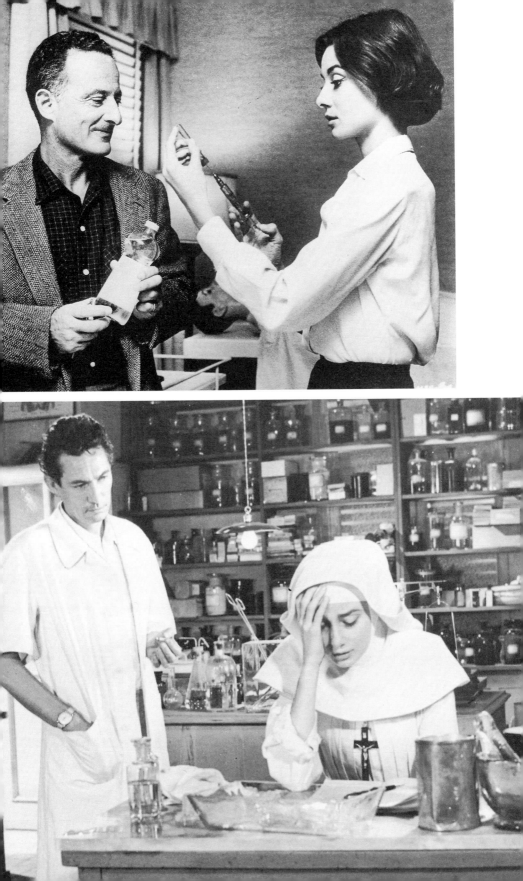

*Love In The Afternoon And
A Nun In The Belgian Congo*

charts in 1959, it having been almost twenty years since *The Song of Bernadette* last made Catholicism commercial. True, this was also to be the Broadway year of *The Sound of Music*, but *The Nun's Story* was a world away from raindrops and roses and hills alive with the sound of singing sisters. It was a somewhat dour account of a Belgian nun trying to suppress her sexuality by good works in the Congo, where Peter Finch was to be found as the 'fallen' doctor out of some minor Graham Greeneland fiction; but Mel Ferrer's enthusiasm for the novel, and its parallels with Audrey's own wartime experience in Belgium and Holland, soon convinced her that this was the movie to do next. Just as well, since without her name above the title it would in all likelihood never have been made. Around her, the director Fred Zinnemann built a rare cast: not only Finch in one of his finest performances, but Peggy Ashcroft, Edith Evans and Mildred Dunnock as mothers more or less superior, and the general feeling that this was to be a 'class' production, despite its apparent lack of immediate box-office appeal.

The project was viewed with an equal amount of unease by the Catholic Church, since the story of a nun who, after seventeen years, loses her vocation was not exactly an ideal recruiting theme; but what both Zinnemann and Hepburn had seen here was the film's humanist potential, the universality of a dilemma about the discovery of self at all costs – 'If I am not for myself,' as Sister Luke asks, 'who will be for me? And if I am for myself alone, what am I?'

Looking back on the filming after thirty years, Zinnemann recalled that 'with the exception of Ingrid Bergman, Audrey was the only possible casting: she was shy, coltish and intelligent. She looked delicate, but there was a hint of iron in the jawline that signified a stubborn will. I thought she would be ideal . . . there's a fine, firm line of development in her performance; it is put together out of dozens of moments of independence. I have never seen anyone more disciplined,

THE *NUN'S STORY*: WITH ZINNEMANN

ON LOCATION IN AFRICA

Love In The Afternoon And
A Nun In The Belgian Congo

more gracious, or more dedicated to her work than Audrey. There was
no ego, no asking for extra favours: there was the greatest considera-
tion for her co-workers. The only thing she requested in the Congo,
where the temperature hovered around ninety-five degrees and the
humidity was incredible, was an air-conditioner. One was promptly
sent from Warners' in Burbank but did not seem to do much good; on
closer inspection it turned out to be a humidifier.'

Initial reaction to *The Nun's Story* was mixed: the budget had
run to three and a half million dollars, very high by the figures of the
day, and there was doubt about the box-office potential: one California
publicist suggested to Zinnemann that his picture might do better if they
retitled it *I Kicked the Habit*. But as usual the experts were proved
wrong: *The Nun's Story* attracted immediately respectful reviews, and
on its first day of release a line had formed around the cavernous Radio
City Music Hall where it was premièred in New York. In Britain, Dilys
Powell wrote of Audrey's 'delicate and devoted performance,' while
Stanley Kauffman noted 'what makes her so right for the part is that,
after she has done all she can with knowledge and design, her beauty
speaks for her; it serves as an intensifying glass for the inner travail she
is trying to convey.'

Another Oscar eluded her here, as was to be the case for the rest
of her career, though *The Nun's Story* did bring her the New York Critics'
and the Best British Actress Awards for 1959. By the time those were
announced, she was deeply involved in another location project, this one
only marginally less arduous than *The Nun's Story*.

WITH HER BELOVED TERRIER, 'FAMOUS'

LUST IN THE DUST: *THE UNFORGIVEN*

Chapter Eight

GREEN MANSIONS AND THE UNFORGIVEN

66

Some of my pictures I just don't care for, but the one with Audrey is

the only one I actually have to turn off when it comes on television.

JOHN HUSTON

99

By the end of the 1950s, Audrey Hepburn could look back on a remarkable, indeed unique run of movies: since *Roman Holiday* in 1953 she had made five pictures, every one of which had got its money back at the box-office and on only one, *Love in the Afternoon*, had reviews for her been less than ecstatic. The list ran from *Sabrina Fair* through *War and Peace* to *Funny Face* and *The Nun's Story*: high-society comedies, Fred Astaire musicals, international epics, serious dramas, she'd done them all in less than seven years from a standing start. Of no other star could the same be said, and it was just about inevitable that the run of luck would have to change, as it did, abruptly, with her next two pictures.

Green Mansions And The Unforgiven

The first of these was the only one she ever made with her husband as director. *Green Mansions* was a novel by W. H. Hudson, subtitled 'A Romance of the Tropical Forest' and largely concerned with an explorer in the Venezuela of the late nineteenth century falling in love with a strange bird-woman called Rima, who eventually gets burned to death as an evil spirit by Indians because she is 'too perfect to live'.

The screenplay had been around a bit, variously considered by Dolores del Rio in the 1940s and Pier Angeli in the early 1950s before being taken up by Ferrer for Audrey. Mel had always been fascinated by the life of the jungle, and saw in *Green Mansions* something rather more significant and poetic than a variation on the meeting of Tarzan and Jane. What he saw, here as in the Broadway *Ondine*, was another 'elfin spirit' role tailor-made for his wife, and despite the fact that his only other movies as a director (*Vendetta*, *The Secret Fury* and *Girl of the Limberlost*) had all proved disappointments at the box-office, he still managed to get this one funded by MGM on the basis of Audrey as Rima the bird-woman. To play the explorer, Ferrer hired the young and promising Anthony Perkins, and around them were gathered such vintage character men as Lee J. Cobb, Nehemiah Persoff and Sessue Hayakawa.

None of them, however, could save *Green Mansions* from going down in flames: the sight of Audrey and Tony Perkins romping around in the undergrowth proved curiously uneasy, and matters were not helped during the studio shooting when Audrey, who had only just learned how to drive, crashed into a parked car at the side of the road. Its occupant, a small-part actress called Joan Lora, subsequently sued for back and neck injuries, claiming fifty thousand dollars and settling after several years for five; the experience did however cure Audrey of ever wanting to drive again.

Green Mansions And The Unforgiven

'*Green Mansions* was not a complete flop in my mind,' said Ferrer some years later, but it was almost everywhere else. Not even the devotion in which Audrey was still held by her fans could persuade them that this had been anything other than a marital mistake. Nobody actually accused her of that of course; moviegoers simply stayed away in polite thousands, waiting for her to come back to them in something rather more suitable or entertaining. As a film, it was best summed up by Penelope Gilliatt for the *Observer*:

'It is hard to associate this artless Hollywood whimsy with the original novel of a serious naturalist and writer: its story, set in wild country south of the Orinoco, has to do with the flight of a young Venezuelan from revolutionaries: his mission is to slay one Rima, daughter of a water spirit and witch of the wildwood. Ploddingly, Anthony Perkins goes about his mission only to find that the witch is none other than Audrey Hepburn, fetchingly clad in a pale nightgown. She is a very nice girl and very kind to animals. Frequently she communes with her dead mother; "Oh mother, hear me, it's about this young man in the forest." Love between these young people is however clearly doomed from the outset, and as their director, Mr Ferrer seems chiefly concerned to lead his wife lovingly and very slowly from pool to pool, tree to tree and frond to frond.'

Audrey was only once again to work with her husband, eight years later on *Wait Until Dark*, and then he would only function as producer; in the meantime, it must have seemed like a good career move to turn towards a rather more experienced director such as John Huston, who was now casting around for someone to play Burt Lancaster's half-breed sister in *The Unforgiven*.

The auguries here were very good indeed: with Lillian Gish, Audie Murphy and Charles Bickford already cast, this was clearly going to be an upmarket affair, and Huston paid Audrey the

Green Mansions And The Unforgiven

ultimate compliment: 'she's as good as the other Hepburn,' with whom he had of course made *The African Queen*. Shooting was to take place in the Durango region of Mexico, and Huston decided that he would pull out all the stops: 'more horses, more bodies, more action than ever before.' The result went way over the top: Audrey got thrown by a high-spirited stallion and had to retire to bed for three weeks, thereby adding several hundred thousand dollars to the budget, and even Huston felt guilty:

'Some of the things that happened on *The Unforgiven* are painful to remember: while we were shooting in Durango, Audrey fell off a horse and fractured a vertebra in her back. I felt responsible, having put her on a horse for the very first time. No matter that she had a good teacher, was brought on slowly, and turned out to be a natural rider. When her horse bolted and some idiot tried to stop it by throwing up his arms, her fall was on my conscience.'

Ferrer was livid on his wife's behalf, and the location seemed for a while to be jinxed, as Audie Murphy nearly drowned after a boat overturned on a lake; Murphy couldn't swim, and had to be rescued by the photographer Inge Morath (later Mrs Arthur Miller) who saw the accident through her telephoto lens and swam out to get him back safely to shore.

'But in the end,' added Huston with his customary laconic wit, 'the worst thing of all to happen was the movie itself: despite some good performances, the overall tone is bombastic and over-inflated. Everybody in it is bigger than life.'

His opinion was shared by most critics, and Audrey's affair with the Great Outdoors ended after these two pictures; the twelve she had still to make, with the obvious exception of *Robin and Marian*, would be decidedly more elegant, indoor affairs with seldom a glimpse of nature in the raw.

Green Mansions And The Unforgiven

'That Huston cannot get a good performance out of Burt Lancaster can hardly be held against him,' Stanley Kauffman wrote of *The Unforgiven*, 'but he has achieved here what no other director has ever managed: to get a really bad performance out of the lovely Audrey Hepburn.'

Back home in Switzerland, at the chalet they had bought in Burgenstock, this was a bleak time for Audrey and Mel: he was still smarting from the shock the critical reaction to *Green Mansions* had given to his self-confidence as a director and the manager of Audrey's career, while she, desperate still to have their baby, suffered yet another miscarriage as a result of her fall on *The Unforgiven* location. Everything was put on hold as she fought to keep herself from the nervous breakdown to which it seemed she would at any moment succumb. There were murmurs of a new Hitchcock thriller, never realized, and even that she might join the queue of actresses eager to take on *Cleopatra* in Rome before the role of the Queen of the Nile finally fell to Elizabeth Taylor.

Hepburn's career was now something of a problem: she was getting three hundred thousand dollars a movie, and there was as yet no sign of any falling away in her devoted audience around the world. But two major flops in a row had not been an asset, and Audrey's determination to stay amid the Swiss Alps, far from all the politics of Hollywood, meant that she had few contacts within the studio system who were eagerly alert for scripts that might suit her better than her recent roles. Like her namesake, nicknamed Katharine of Arrogance by Hollywood for her determination to reside in New York, Audrey was also regarded as an outsider with few if any loyalties to the old studio chiefs, and they in their turn were not about to offer any support should her career start to slide. Indeed there was almost a feeling that they would welcome it, as

proof of the impossibility of any sustained star survival outside the Hollywood system.

But as it happened, all such professional considerations were put to one side when, less than six months after her latest miscarriage, she got the news she had been waiting for: once again she was pregnant, and this time she was taking no risks of any kind. While Mel went on working as an actor, she spent the next six months at home in Burgenstock 'like a cloistered woman, counting the hours until my baby is born.' Sure enough and safe enough, Sean Ferrer was born at the maternity clinic in Lucerne on 17 January 1960, and christened a few days later in a specially-made Givenchy robe. Movies that Audrey had turned down while awaiting him included *West Side Story* and *The Cardinal*, but the exchange seemed more than worth it: 'To my shame,' she said years later, 'I have to admit that I have never taken acting that seriously, but motherhood is something altogether different. From the time I was a little girl, from the earliest time I can remember, the thing I most wanted was babies and my miscarriages were more painful to me than anything ever, including my parents' divorce and the disappearance of my father. From the time I had Sean, I hung onto my marriage because of him, and more and more I began to resent the time I spent away from him on location. I guess I was just born to be a mother, and if I could have had more than my two sons, if I could have had daughters as well and dozens of them, then I certainly would.'

And in the end of course she did: all the children world-wide of Unicef were Audrey's children, as Sean himself noted when accepting his mother's humanitarian Oscar a few weeks after she died.

WITH MEL AT THE BIRTH OF THEIR ONLY CHILD, SEAN, IN JANUARY 1960

Our huckleberry friend;

HOLLY GOLIGHTLY IN *BREAKFAST AT TIFFANY'S* (1961)

·104·

Chapter Nine

OUR HUCKLEBERRY FRIEND

66

Give me a list of the fifty richest men in Brazil

regardless of colour or race; I have dined with twenty-six

different rats during the last month alone; any guy with

class will give you fifty bucks for the cab, I usually ask

another fifty for the John as well.

HOLLY GOLIGHTLY

99

O f all the roles played by Audrey Hepburn, from the Princess of *Roman Holiday* through *Sabrina Fair* and *Funny Face* all the way to Eliza Doolittle, Holly Golightly is at once the most charismatic and the most haunting. She was the invention of the novelist Truman Capote, though, as always with Truman, invention was not quite the word. At best, he was a photo-journalist who used words instead of cameras; his characters nearly all came in some shape or form from real life and usually his own. Thus the models for Holly were half a dozen of the stylish girls-about-town that Truman had already come across on his travels around New York's Upper East Side, among them Oona O'Neill (later Mrs Charles Chaplin), Carol Marcus (later Mrs Walter Matthau), Gloria Vanderbilt and Doris Lilly. As Capote's biographer Gerald Clarke has noted,

'Holly lives the Capote philosophy that his other characters only dream about: her whole life is an expression of freedom and an acceptance of human irregularities, her own as well as everyone else's. The only sin she recognizes is hypocrisy: she is a woman who makes a holiday of life, through which she walks lightly . . . . She shares Truman's fears and anxieties as well, the "mean reds" as she calls them. For her the cure is to jump in a cab and head for Tiffany's, where nothing bad could happen "amid that lovely smell of silver and alligator wallets," hence her dream to have breakfast in that soothing setting.'

When Audrey died, branches of Tiffany around the world put her photograph in the window in one of their silver frames, so totally had she become identified with the store. Yet she was by no means the first choice for the film: Truman himself had wanted Marilyn Monroe, who he said 'would have been absolutely marvellous, and wanted it so badly that she worked up two whole scenes all by herself to play for me. She was terrifically good, but Paramount double-crossed me in every way and cast Audrey. She is an old friend and one of my favourite people, but she was just wrong for that part and the whole movie became a mawkish valentine to her talent.'

What Hepburn did to Holly can clearly be seen if you compare the movie to the original novella: she anaesthetized her.

'We're after the same rainbow's end, waiting round the bend...'

Our Huckleberry Friend

Truman's Holly is a call-girl with a heart of platinum and gold: Audrey's is an infinitely purer soul, devoid of the earthy sexuality that is in every line of the book. But for a mere sixty-five thousand dollars Capote had sold all rights in his story to Paramount, who in turn brought in George Axelrod to clean it up for a mass screen audience in the days when that was still thought advisable.

As a result, the original Holly's life and language were considerably altered on her route through Hollywood: the marriage at age fourteen is legally annulled, the eleven lovers have disappeared and though she is still a call-girl of the very best kind, she now has honest motives for her prostitution. Like Sally Bowles in *Cabaret*, Holly has come a long way from her origins on the printed page.

But something about the elegance of the original was still there, not only in Hepburn's stunningly enchanting performance but even in the New York skyscrapers as filmed by Blake Edwards: at a time when Manhattan movies were already getting more grainy and realistic, this was an unashamed throwback to the days of *On The Town*, the dreamy New York of soaring lilac-and-gold avenues, reflections in shop windows and Sondheim's *Ladies Who Lunch*. The city looks sunny, sparkling and elegant instead of grimly Third World, and, as Dilys Powell noted, though the film lost the sharp gin-and-vermouth tang of the novella, it gained in Audrey Hepburn 'a sentimental fantasy, one of Lautrec's poster-women with a broken heart, who becomes for the film a creature of high spirits and delicate sensibilities, discipline and spontaneity. She bewitches us into acceptance; her extravagant, lovely clothes and her absurd, artificial mannerisms, the sophistication and the heartbreak fuse into a figure which, within the confines of the

THE TIFFANY TRIANGLE: PATRICIA NEAL, AUDREY, AND GEORGE PEPPARD

IN THE RAIN WITH GEORGE PEPPARD AFTER THE REDISCOVERY OF CAT

screen, is all alive. Not even the excusably morose no-name cat who is
her constant companion can look more persuasive: without her this
might well not have worked, but with her the film affords a pleasure
which is refined but not attenuated. The American cinema still has a
good deal to offer.'

A strong cast also included George Peppard, Patricia Neal,
Martin Balsam and Mickey Rooney as Holly's manic Japanese neigh-
bour, but this was and will always be Hepburn's film: she is in almost
every frame of it, and when huskily she croons Mercer-Mancini's *Moon
River* from the tenement staircase of her apartment building, the
sequence becomes one of the most romantic in the whole history of
Hollywood. The darker shades of *Tiffany's*, such as the suggestion that
the Patricia Neal who is keeping George Peppard might in her true sexuality be more interested in Holly, are carefully airbrushed out of
Blake Edwards's glossy crowd-pleasing comedy of appalling manners,
which explains why Truman Capote was always to be so irritable about
the greatest commercial success his work was ever to achieve. Wacky,
dizzy and kooky, Holly was the perfect cinema icon for 1961, but she
was no longer Capote's more complex or uneasy figure: she had been
softened and straightened out for the silver screen, just another example of Hepburn as Princess.

After a couple of flops the success of *Breakfast at Tiffany's* re-
established Audrey's screen career, which was still under the careful
management of Mel Ferrer. By maintaining the family home at
Burgenstock, hurrying back there as soon as shooting stopped, and
resolutely refusing to buy or even rent homes in California or New
York, the Ferrers were able to maintain an almost regal exile from, and
indifference to, the Hollywood machine. Though she would from time
to time consent to major fashion-shoots for Givenchy, Hepburn would
only ever give the most banal and unrevealing of on-set interviews,

usually demanding that all questions be submitted in writing and in advance. A tough negotiator was already hiding beneath her Peter Pan exterior: the survivor of Arnhem did not find it too difficult to see off any American journalists or studio executives who thought she might deal with them on anything other than her own terms and territory, with the result that she commanded a kind of wary respect denied to those stars who actually lived within hailing distance of the studios. Hepburn was perceived as foreign royalty and treated accordingly, not with love but with the grudging acknowledgement that she was nobody's play-as-cast studio property. Even before the old Hollywood contract system had started to crumble, Hepburn was one of the very first of the independents, able to negotiate freelance contracts for one picture at a time and to refuse any of the more tacky assignments still being doled out to the likes of Marilyn Monroe and Natalie Wood.

She was also sharp enough in her choice of roles never to get typecast: after the glossy elegance of *Breakfast at Tiffany's*, she realized the time had come to get back into serious drama and the one she chose brought her back to William Wyler, who had made her a star in *Roman Holiday*. There was nothing escapist or glossy about *The Children's Hour*: it was a remake of *We Three*, a film Wyler had made in 1937 from the Lillian Hellman play about school teachers falsely accused of lesbianism by a vicious pupil. The first version had only been able to hint at the play's true theme, but by 1961 it was reckoned that audiences could just about handle the topic, especially as the new casting was to co-star Audrey with Shirley MacLaine, also then appearing on all box-office listings of the top five female film stars in the world: the other three, for the record, were Doris Day, Elizabeth Taylor and Marilyn Monroe.

But Wyler was past his *Roman Holiday* prime, and *The Children's Hour* was a limp affair, nominated and then bypassed in five

On the paramount set

WITH JAMES GARNER ON THE SET OF *THE CHILDREN'S HOUR* (1961)
WHICH WAS THE SECOND OF HER THREE FILMS FOR WILLIAM WYLER (THE
OTHERS WERE *ROMAN HOLIDAY* AND *HOW TO STEAL A MILLION*)

Our Huckleberry Friend

Oscar categories. It was hoped that MacLaine would teach Hepburn, already dubbed 'the Princess', how to curse and Audrey in turn would teach Shirley how to dress. Neither wish was fulfilled.

Audrey returned to her preferred role as a wife and mother; still desperately thin and waif-like, she had her heart set on a large earth-mother family and would give herself anything up to a year between movies to see if there was any chance of another pregnancy. Hepburn never had to act in order to define herself: though never less than professional on the set, and regally kind to all its workers, she had no particular love for movie-making and no particular desire to be in the eye of the camera for longer than it took to make a movie. Though once passionate about the possibility of becoming a ballet dancer, she was never really that keen on the life of an actress or indeed a film star. But nor did she have unlimited private means, and from time to time there were still contracts that had to be signed; by and large, she worked on past form. If the director was distinguished and the co-stars reasonably interesting, she would make the movie: a European location was a bonus, and if the film was to be set in her beloved Paris, then that usually proved the clincher.

Those were high demands, and not easy to fulfil: after *The Children's Hour* she waited almost a year before anything even remotely attractive could tempt her away from the Swiss chalet. But then, almost simultaneously, came the offer of two comedies, both set in Paris, one to co-star her old *Sabrina Fair* friend William Holden and the other to co-star the actor with whom more than any other she had always wanted to play: Cary Grant. The movies had Audrey and Paris in common, but that was it: they were in fact to be by general reckoning respectively the worst and the best that she ever made, and the worst came first.

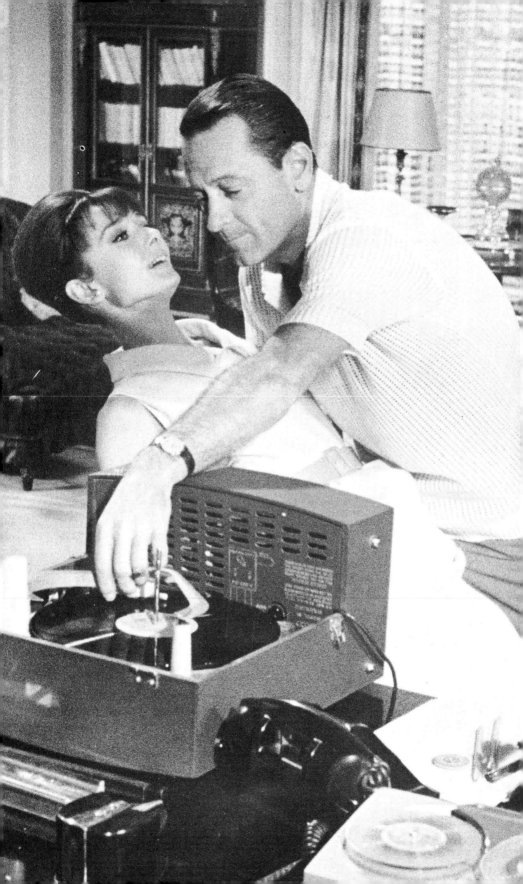

Chapter Ten

I COULD HAVE DANCED ALL NIGHT

66

My Fair Lady was an ordeal and when it was over

I virtually broke down from exhaustion: still, they paid me

a million dollars for it, and I was, I think, only the second

actress after Elizabeth Taylor to get that for one movie.

99

'I remember,' Bill Holden told Ryan O'Neal once, 'the day that I arrived at Orly Airport to make *Paris When It Sizzles*. I could hear my footsteps echoing against the walls of the transit corridor, just like a condemned man walking the last mile. I realized that I had to face Audrey again, and that I had to deal with my drinking, and I didn't think I could handle either situation.'

Holden had never entirely recovered from the unrequited romantic passion he had developed for Audrey on the set of *Sabrina*

'*P*ARIS WHEN IT SIZZLES IS HOLLYWOOD WHEN IT FIZZLES' :

*N*EW YORK HERALD TRIBUNE

I Could Have Danced All Night

Fair a decade earlier, and they were now to be reunited in rather less happy circumstances. Both stars still owed Paramount one picture each, and the studio had decided to bring them together with the director Richard Quine for the English-language remake of a 1954 French Julien Duvivier comedy called *La Fête d'Henriette*, about a screenwriter who hires a young secretary to act out the fantasies of his filmscripts in the hope that she might be the inspiration to help him finish them. But Holden was in no fit state for a comedy, and although the screenplay was by the same George Axelrod who had recently transformed *Breakfast at Tiffany's* for the cinema, this was one of his most leaden efforts. As if realizing the trouble they were in, the producers signed up an amazing roster of 'guest stars': Noël Coward, Tony Curtis, Marlene Dietrich and Audrey's husband Mel Ferrer, none of whom could rescue a picture of stunning inadequacy and uneasiness. '*Paris When It Sizzles* is Hollywood when it fizzles,' noted the *New York Herald Tribune*, and it was more than lucky for Audrey that she was able, still in Paris, to move on to a script that was vastly more entertaining and distinguished.

This was a comedy thriller by Peter Stone called *Charade* which had attracted the attention of the Stanley Donen for whom Audrey had worked so happily in Paris on *Funny Face*. This time there was to be no singing or dancing, but Donen was also a favourite director of Cary Grant and he it was who finally managed to put together the 'dream ticket' casting of Cary and Audrey for the first and only time.

CHARADE (1963): 'IN SPITE OF HER FRAGILE APPEARANCE

SHE'S LIKE STEEL,' SAID CARY GRANT, 'SHE MAY BEND, BUT SHE NEVER BREAKS'

HEPBURN ON THE RUN FROM HOLDEN IN *PARIS*

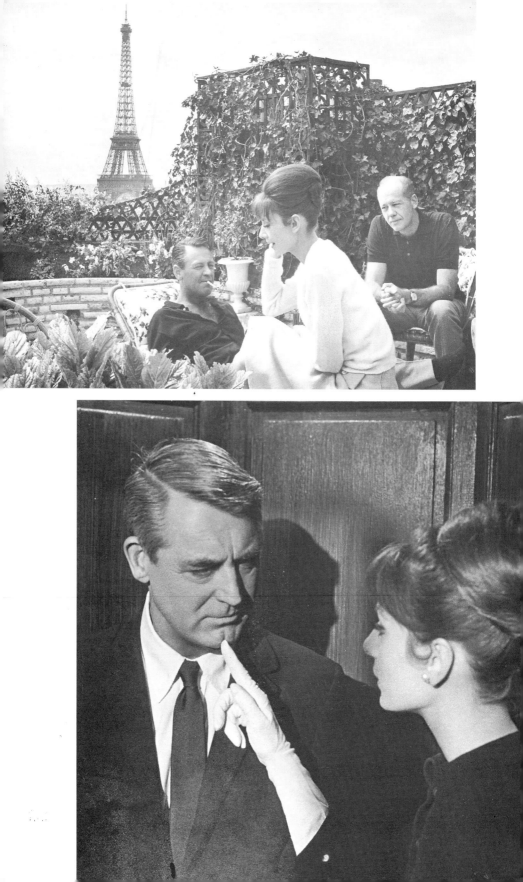

I Could Have Danced All Night

Grant was expert in two fields: at precisely this kind of stylish whodunnit, as usually directed by Hitchcock, and at working opposite ice-maidens like Ingrid Bergman, Grace Kelly and now Audrey, who would melt but only under the right temperature of flame, which he alone seemed able to assess. True, he was already old enough at sixty to be Hepburn's father; but she who had already worked with Peck, Bogart, Holden, Cooper and Astaire had always been determined to add Cary to her list of leading men, and there could be no better opportunity.

Donen as producer and director surrounded them with an expert cast of character men led by Walter Matthau, James Coburn and George Kennedy, and as a caper-comedy-thriller *Charade* perfectly caught, indeed defined, this early 1960s genre: a film which sends itself up even while delivering some of its best surprises.

Indeed the only unhappiness around the whole set, apart from occasional moments of uneasiness between Audrey and Cary as to who was getting the best photo-coverage in the local press, was the sudden realization by Hepburn that she was filming on precisely the same set and with much of the same furniture as had been used for *Love in the Afternoon*: the ghost of the recently deceased Gary Cooper seemed somehow very real to her as the new film moved towards its climax.

Any brief temperamental battles with Grant were however soon forgotten: 'Working with Cary is so simple,' said Audrey,

---

*P*ARIS WHEN IT SIZZLES (1964), AUDREY WITH CO-STAR WILLIAM HOLDEN,

STILL HOPELESSLY IN LOVE WITH HER, AND THEIR DIRECTOR RICHARD QUINE

'*C*ARY WOULD NEVER KISS ME IN THE FILM, BECAUSE HE SAID HE WAS FAR TOO OLD;'

HE ALWAYS HAD GREAT TASTE, AND NOBODY EVER NOTICES THERE WASN'T ANY KISSING

AUDREY ON THEIR *CHARADE*

I Could Have Danced All Night

'because he does all the acting and all you have to do is react,' while for his part Cary responded 'that girl mothered our entire Paris company. The day she left the set we were bereft: we had to stick around for the fight scenes without her, and we were absolutely lost.'

But the greatest gift Cary gave Audrey was, indirectly, her next role. Jack Warner had for five years now had the rights to film Lerner and Loewe's hugely successful stage musical of *Pygmalion* – *My Fair Lady* – and the studio had set its heart on Cary Grant for Professor Higgins; despite the triumph that Rex Harrison had enjoyed in the role on Broadway and in the West End, Grant was felt to be better box-office. He was however playing very hard to get, not least because of his own reservations about his ability to master the kind of spoken singing which Harrison had used so effectively to land individual words on pitch. If however he were ever to agree to the role, Grant added, his ideal Eliza would be Audrey Hepburn.

Warner and his director George Cukor had already decided that they too would like Audrey, since it was believed that Julie Andrews, having never made a film, would be unlikely to sell any cinema seats, a theory she rapidly disproved with *Mary Poppins* and *The Sound of Music*. Audrey thus already had Warners' where she wanted them: if they were to use her as a bait to attract Grant, she could virtually name her own price for Eliza, and she did. One million dollars, a sum that had been paid to Liz Taylor for *Cleopatra* but to no other actress in the whole history of Hollywood.

A whole roster of other actors, among them George Sanders, Noël Coward, Michael Redgrave and Rock Hudson, had been

THE LAST OF HER GREAT DIRECTORS: WITH GEORGE CUKOR ON THE SET OF
MY FAIR LADY (1964)

I Could Have Danced All Night

considered for Higgins, but in the end it was Grant himself who gave Cukor and Warner the courage they needed to settle for the original stage casting. 'Not only will I not make your film,' he finally told them, 'but unless you keep Rex Harrison as Higgins, I won't even go see it.' And so they did: Cecil Beaton was again to be the designer, Stanley Holloway was to repeat his splendidly rambunctious Alfred Doolittle, Wilfrid Hyde-White was to be Colonel Pickering and by the time it started shooting in early 1963 it was already evident that this was to be the musical of the decade and perhaps the last of its high-style, big-budget studio kind, coming in at just over seventeen million dollars.

There was just one little problem: despite her lighthearted, enchanting singing of *Funny Face* and *Moon River*, Lerner and Loewe decided that Audrey's voice was simply not up to the demands of their score and that she should be dubbed by Marni Nixon, who had performed much the same chore for Deborah Kerr on *The King and I* and for Natalie Wood on *West Side Story*. But this decision, taken when shooting was already well under way, severely undermined Audrey's confidence in herself; incredibly, considering her post-war life in London, she also had to take pronunciation lessons on her cockney accent for the early scenes.

Relations on the set were always somewhat tense: Rex Harrison was never the most generous of co-stars and, having already played the role for two years on Broadway and another one in London, was in no mood to accommodate a new partner, especially after he discovered that, at two hundred and fifty thousand dollars, his salary would amount to just a quarter of what Warners were paying Audrey.

Then again, there was the problem of the on-set relationship between the director George Cukor and the designer Cecil Beaton: both gay egomaniacs, they each regarded Audrey as their personal property and would alternately bicker and feud over whether Cecil's

'ALL I WANT IS A ROOM SOMEWHERE, FAR AWAY FROM THE COLD NIGHT AIR...'

AS ELIZA IN *MY FAIR LADY*

I Could Have Danced All Night

stills (he was also working on a book of photographs of the filming) were getting in the way of George's shots, or vice versa.

Through all of this, Audrey maintained her usual reserved charm and distant, elegant friendship to cast and crew alike, but there was now another problem: the marriage to Ferrer, which had not been stable for several months, was exposed to European press rumours that he was seeing other actresses on other pictures while Audrey was serving her long summer on *My Fair Lady*. Thus what should have been the happiest of films for her, directed by the most famously sensitive 'women's director' in Hollywood and designed by Beaton who, with his photographer's eye, had been one of the very first to see her potential back in the London of 1949, became an oddly uneasy one, overshadowed by Harrison's hostility, Ferrer's other interests and worst of all, as the shooting dragged on into the autumn of 1963, news of the killing of President Kennedy which a distraught Audrey had to break to the unit in a tearful speech.

But the picture had started rather more rosily, as Beaton noted in his diary: 'Audrey is a natural: she has taken up her role in life with a complete ease that is rare. She is strong and firm in character, and seems never to be swayed to do the foolish or unkind thing. Her relationship with Mel is not all that easy, but she loves him: Audrey takes the rough with the smooth, and there is a great deal of the smooth. Her success is astonishing, and not only financially, yet she never allows herself to regard it except as her professional career; it comes second always to her private life, and the infinite trouble and finesse she manages in that strike me as being extraordinary.'

WITH DAME GLADYS COOPER AS MRS HIGGINS

I Could Have Danced All Night

And Hepburn repaid the compliment: 'Dearest CB,' she wrote after he had shown her some of his early costume sketches and photographs of how she would look in them, 'ever since I can remember I have always so badly wanted to be beautiful, and looking at your photographs I saw that for at least a short time I am, all because of you.'

Later, finding herself in the cross-fire between Cukor and Beaton, Audrey seems to have withdrawn a little from Cecil's devoted gaze, but he still ended his book about the filming with his own delight at 'there being no one better to dress in all the world than the impeccable Audrey Hepburn.' For Audrey herself, who had told Cecil at the onset 'this one is the mountain top, they won't get any better so let's make sure that we really enjoy ourselves', that proved a little harder than anticipated. The veteran Henry Daniell, star of many a Cukor picture, actually keeled over dead at her feet during one of the ballroom scenes, and Audrey began to feel that in some way the film was jinxed, if not by 'the curse of Julie Andrews' (who had not been allowed to repeat her stage success on film), then by some malevolent studio spirit. And that uneasiness manifests itself in aspects of Hepburn's work here: though *My Fair Lady* turns up with increasing regularity on television as one of the last great Hollywood musicals, its highlights really belong to the trio of English character actors (Harrison, Stanley Holloway and Wilfrid Hyde-White) rather than the Fair Lady herself, who often seems distinctly uneasy in her Covent Garden sequences and not much happier in the Higgins homestead. Most Elizas, in the original *Pygmalion* and in the musical, have usually been at their best either before or after her translation to high society: Audrey is alone in seeming unhappy on both sides of it.

As if reflecting that unease, the voters of the Oscar Academy in 1964 declined to give her a second award: instead they required her to present one to Rex Harrison and, to add to her humiliation,

THE LAST GREAT GATHERING OF THAT HOLLYWOOD RAJ OF
EXPATRIATE BRITISH CHARACTER ACTORS:
REX HARRISON AND STANLEY HOLLOWAY WITH AUDREY ON THE
SET OF *MY FAIR LADY*

W E'VE GROWN ACCUSTOMED TO HER FACE

I Could Have Danced All Night

gave their 'best actress' Oscar to Julie Andrews for *Mary Poppins*. Characteristically, Audrey beamed throughout the ceremony, was first to congratulate Rex and Julie, and never in public or private gave any indication that she was less than delighted at the outcome. The problem of her performance was perhaps best defined by Philip Oakes, reviewing the film for the *Sunday Telegraph*:

'It has an over-abundance of sweetness and light, and the casting of Audrey Hepburn is a classic case of gilding the lily until its petals wilt. On stage the part was played by Julie Andrews, a talented girl but not, at the time, a world name. Miss Hepburn is splendidly equipped in this aspect and in many others, but she labours under one major handicap: she doesn't sing. In the film her songs are dubbed, devoid of credit, by Marni Nixon and although miming to a canned voice has long been a tradition of film musicals, I still find the sight of a beautiful dummy singing someone else's head off rather less than enthralling.'

It was Jack Warner himself who delivered the final insult, assuring journalists on Oscar night that he had voted for Julie Andrews instead of his own candidate: those who had noted in the past that Audrey's devotion to Hollywood was less than passionate could now reflect that she had some cause to keep her European distance whenever possible. As a rule, she was from now on to make pictures as far away from California as the laws of international movie-making would allow.

And it was the chance of getting back to her beloved Paris that brought her a few months later to *How To Steal A Million*, the last of the three films that she would make with the William Wyler

HOME AGAIN IN SWITZERLAND: MEL, SEAN, AUDREY 1965

HOW TO STEAL A MILLION (1966) AND A FAREWELL TO WILLY WYLER

WITH PETER O'TOOLE STEALING A MILLION: 'THERE WAS A MODESTY AND SADNESS,' HE SAID, 'BEHIND HER STERN AND FORMIDABLE FACADE'

I Could Have Danced All Night

who had first given her stardom in *Roman Holiday*. This was a typical if over-long caper comedy of the period, one which would co-star her with Peter O'Toole, still so hot from *Lawrence of Arabia* that he had even been a contender for *My Fair Lady* on screen.

In truth she and Ferrer had been hoping to do something together to shore up their patchy marriage: a movie about the Empress Joséphine, maybe, or even the *Peter Pan* they had so often discussed. But when Disney made it clear they were never to get the *Pan* screen rights, and the money Ferrer needed for *Joséphine* was nowhere to be found, Hepburn decided she might as well go back to Wyler and Paris and a script that could have been almost entirely made up of offcuts from such earlier Audrey vehicles as *Roman Holiday*, *Gigi*, *Sabrina Fair*, *Charade* and even *Love in the Afternoon*. The story, originally entitled *Venus Rising*, was of an old art forger (Hugh Griffith in the best role of the film) whose daughter persuades a high-society thief (O'Toole) to steal one of his works from a museum before its fakery can be discovered.

Once again the filming was not exactly easy: George C. Scott was abruptly fired from the set for being late and replaced by Eli Wallach, and the pairing of O'Toole and Hepburn produced the traditional gossip-column speculation as to their off-screen relationship, which was in actuality never more than reasonably friendly. Bosley Crowther for the *New York Times* found the movie 'as preposterous as the gaily eccentric wardrobe of Givenchy costumes that Miss Hepburn wears,' while *Time* felt that 'in a film that cries for wild hilarity and a heady spirit of adventure, everything happens according to long-established rules from the first skittish encounter to the last eager kiss.' *Newsweek* even risked critical *lèse-majesté* by daring to attack Audrey herself for 'trading rather too heavily on her usual selection of charm.'

Chapter Eleven

TWO FOR THE ROAD AND THE END OF A MARRIAGE

66

I thought a marriage between two good and loving people

had to last until one of them died: I can't tell you how hard

we tried, and how disillusioned I was by our failure: it can't

be easy married to a world celebrity, but I really did put my

career second and still it didn't help at the end.

99

L ife at Burgenstock was not good: Audrey lost yet another baby soon after *How To Steal A Million*, Ferrer was increasingly away on location, and now his wife faced a new problem: her beloved Sean was six, approaching full-time schooling, and

ONE FOR THE ROAD: 1967, IN STANLEY DONEN'S ROMANTIC COMEDY

Two For The Road And The End
Of A Marriage

Burgenstock was in a German-speaking canton of Switzerland. For a survivor of Arnhem to have a son grow up with German as his first language was, to Audrey, unthinkable and intolerable: within months she had moved her family over the Canton borderline into French Switzerland and bought the house at Tolochenaz, where she was to live out the rest of her life and where indeed she was to die twenty-seven years later.

But La Paisible, as the Vaudois farmhouse above the Geneva-Lausanne motorway was hopefully known, needed some expensive refurbishment and, as all the money due from *My Fair Lady* was yet to arrive (it had been contracted on a profits-percentage basis), Audrey soon enough felt the need to get back to work. This was now not quite so easy: the Oscar voters had delivered a considerable slap in the face, the reviews on her last picture had been dire, and the suggestion was that the old-style, high-style, Givenchy-robed caper comedies in which she played the waif-lover to Cary Grant or who-ever had now had their day.

A new reality was overtaking the cinemas by 1967, and if Hepburn was to have any part of it then she would have rapidly to distance herself from a world of ageing matinée idols and highly overdressed sets: she would have to stop seeming a survivor of the glossy 1950s and start belonging to the swinging 1960s, even if they were more than halfway over already.

But how to do it? Hollywood as usual offered no help at all, at least not on home ground, but another of her most faithful directors now came up with a remarkable and adroit solution. Stanley Donen had starred Audrey in both *Funny Face* and *Charade*: by pairing her first with Astaire and then with Grant, he had achieved two of her most successful and beloved movies. But he was the first to see that the world had changed: where Wyler in her last film had tried

Two for the road: ALBERT FINNEY, ROMANTICALLY LINKED TO
AUDREY DURING THE SHOOTING, NOTED AFTERWARDS: 'PLAYING A LOVE SCENE
WITH A WOMAN AS SEXY AS AUDREY LEADS YOU TO THE EDGE
WHERE REALITY AND MAKE-BELIEVE GET BLURRED'

Two For The Road And The End
Of A Marriage

to get back something of the flavour of *Roman Holiday*, Donen now turned his back on a world of elderly charmers and paired her instead with the hottest and roughest young actor to have come out of the Royal Court and the grainy black-and-white North Country movies of the British new wave: her partner for *Two For The Road* was to be Albert Finney. And another thing: the writer was not to be another Hollywood grin-and-gag merchant of the old school but a young Cambridge novelist already renowned for an acerbic, wry line in elegant disillusion and cynicism: Frederic Raphael, writing here an original screenplay about twelve years in the life of a wealthy and trendy couple and their memories of better times as they drive through France.

Where Wyler had tried, without success, to keep Audrey as he had first made her in *Roman Holiday*, hence the overlong, top-heavy failure of *How To Steal A Million*, Donen realized that a complete rethink was called for: no longer would she be dressed by Givenchy, starred against an older charmer and allowed to do her elfin spirit. Instead, *Two For The Road* would reflect all the insecurities of the late 1960s and it was not perhaps the happiest of coincidences that her character in the film should be living out, as she was in real life, the end of a twelve-year marriage.

At thirty Finney was in fact seven years younger than Audrey, but when they made *Two For The Road* their partnership had an edgy, adult tension that was nowhere apparent in her earlier little-girl-lost work: Hepburn had grown up on film at last, and audiences around the world welcomed her new maturity, coming as it did with no loss of screen style.

AUDREY AND ALBERT WITH WILLIAM DANIELS AT THE SIDE OF THE *ROAD*

Two For The Road And The End Of A Marriage

'I really love Albie,' she said during the shooting, and there were few who could doubt it: a sharp, jokey contrast to the somewhat dour, older Ferrer, he seemed to bring out in her a whole new joy which was wonderfully reflected on screen. And maybe off the screen too: William Daniels, the American character actor who joined the film quite late into its schedule, immediately noted that the two stars 'were having a hell of a good time together' and it was as though Audrey had taken on a new lease of life: away from her father-figure and the old Hollywood comedies, she seemed here to be reborn as a European star and to be quite consciously remaking herself. There was however just one problem with all this: Audrey's determination never to lose sight of her son Sean, and more importantly never to risk losing him even for a part of the year to any kind of potential custody battle with Ferrer. So the marriage was to be kept going at all costs: *Two For The Road* and the Finney interlude were to be considered something of a holiday from reality, which may well be what gives the movie a carefree intensity of feeling that had been lacking in her more sterile recent work on *My Fair Lady* and *How To Steal A Million*: on *Two For The Road*, Audrey was back in the land of the living, with all the pain that entailed.

But even before it started, she had agreed to make another movie with Ferrer as its producer: this was *Wait Until Dark*, a long-running Broadway and West End thriller about a blind woman terrorized by murderous drug-smugglers. It was routine, sub-Hitchcock material but Ferrer surrounded her with a strong of 'heavies' (Alan Arkin, Richard Crenna and Jack Weston) and her

WITH MEL AS THEY APPROACHED THE END OF THEIR MARRIAGE

ON THE SET OF *WAIT UNTIL DARK* (1967)

Two For The Road And The End
Of A Marriage

performance was convincing enough to win her another Oscar nomination, though in the event she lost out to Katharine Hepburn and *Guess Who's Coming To Dinner?*

But by the time the filming had ended, so too had the Ferrer marriage: whether the strain of working together again for the first time in almost a decade (since *Green Mansions* in fact) had proved too great, whether there was any truth in the theory that Ferrer was too keen for her to work at a time when she more and more wanted to be at home, or whether a long and difficult relationship had just finally reached the end of the road, it was left to Audrey's mother the Baroness to announce on 20 November 1968 that, despite last-minute attempts at reconciliation, the marriage of her daughter and Mr Ferrer had ended after fourteen years due to 'irreconcilable differences.' To their credit, neither Mel nor Audrey ever talked in public about that divorce, nor indeed in any real detail about the marriage which had preceded it. In later years Audrey would express regret, pain, grief and a curious kind of guilt that she had failed to make it work, as though the entire marriage had been her personal responsibility and failure. Having never really recovered from her parents' divorce, she was never quite to recover from this one either, regarding it in a touching if somewhat impractical fashion as a kind of illness which the best-kept families ought to manage not to catch. She made sure that Sean stayed with her at the Tolochenaz chalet whenever possible, although she also ensured that he was never to lose touch with Mel the way she had lost touch with her father. Like everything else about her life and career, the divorce was organized in an avalanche of good manners, the smile as ever masking the steel below.

WITH HER BELOVED SEAN (1967)

Chapter Twelve

MAD ABOUT
THE BOY

66

Some people think that giving up my career was a great

sacrifice made for my family, but you know it wasn't that

at all: it was what I most wanted to do.

99

W ith the end of the shooting of *Wait Until Dark*, and the end of
the Ferrer marriage, something else ended too: Audrey's life
as a working film star. She would live for another twenty-five years,
but in those years she would make only four more films (*Robin and
Marian, Bloodline, They All Laughed* and *Always*), none of them
anywhere near the top of her movie roll of honour. In one sense it
was already all over: on the eve of her fortieth birthday, she had
already made every great film she was ever going to make, played

THE SECOND MARRIAGE: IN SWITZERLAND AGAIN, JANUARY 1969,

TO DR ANDREA DOTTI

every role that was going to be truly and irrevocably hers, worked with all the great Hollywood stars she was ever going to captivate and bewitch. There was a new movie world out there, a world of grainy reality and naked sex and sudden violence, and she didn't want any part of it.

And so she retreated to the Swiss chalet with Sean, determined that if she could no longer be a wife she could at least be a mother to the son she so loved. But she was not used to living without a husband, and when Sean went off to school the loneliness of Tolochenaz was considerable: within a few months she was making regular trips to visit friends in the Rome she had so enjoyed since her first great film there, and within a few more months there were diary items reporting 'intimate dinners', first with one of the many pretenders to the Spanish throne, Prince Alfonso de Bourbon, and then more frequently with a young and wealthy Italian psychiatrist, Dr Andrea Mario Dotti. Nine years younger than Audrey, and already with the reputation as a womanizer that was to be the eventual destruction of their marriage, Dotti was an expert on many forms of depression, a condition by now all too familiar to Hepburn. Handsome, young, rich, he was the perfect suitor: within six months of their first meeting on a Mediterranean cruise, and only two months after Audrey's divorce from Mel was finalized, they were married in a civil ceremony at Morges on 18 January 1969.

Audrey agreed at once to lead the life of an Italian wife, Signora Dotti, and the two witnesses at her second wedding, the actress Capucine and Yul Brynner's then wife Doris, agreed that

THE NEW BABY, LUCA, BEING WALKED BY AUDREY

AND CAPUCINE, SWITZERLAND 1970

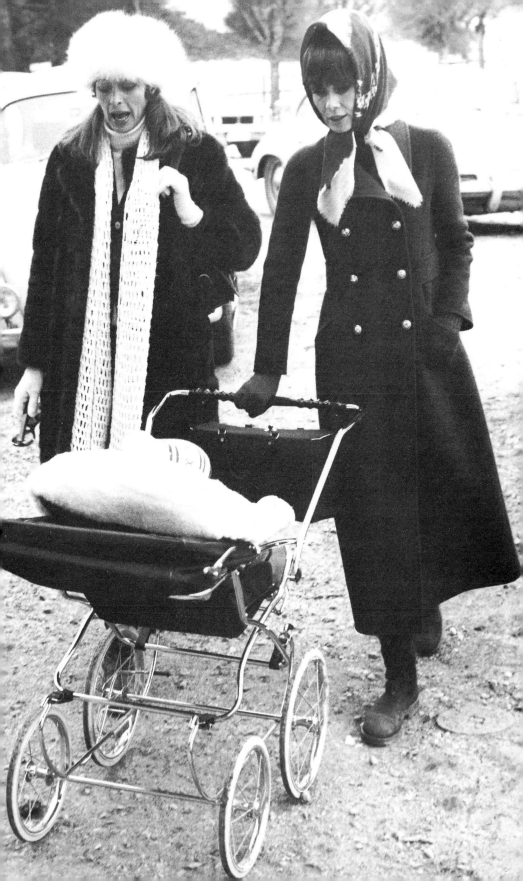

Mad About The Boy

they had never seen her looking more radiant. The plan was simple: to live in Rome with Andrea, and to have the other children she had so longed for during the years with Ferrer. Within four months of the wedding she was pregnant and, determined not to suffer another of the miscarriages which had haunted her in her first marriage, retired to the chalet she was always to keep at Tolochenaz to await the happy event. Whereupon she learnt a sudden and sharp lesson in the difference between an Italian marriage and any other kind: Dr Dotti, with the Signora now out of sight in Switzerland, cheerfully returned to the night-club circuit in Rome and the girlfriends of his past, with whom, to Hepburn's fury, he was regularly photographed in the press. Once again, it seemed, although for very different reasons, Audrey was to be trapped inside a difficult marriage for the sake of the children she still so craved.

Her second son and only other child, Luca Dotti, was born in Lausanne on 8 February 1970 and shortly thereafter Audrey moved back to Rome, having learned that it was not wise to leave Dr Dotti unattended for too long. David Niven, often the best chronicler of Hollywood's private lives, said of Audrey at this time, 'When she was swept off to Rome by Dr Dotti she was, I think, determined just to be a good wife to this very socially minded Roman; she was indeed a wonderful wife to him, but the longer it went on the more people felt that she was just too good for him, and that he took advantage of her, while she just put her career on hold to be with him.'

But other people's marriages are always a foreign country, and for a few years at any rate Audrey was clearly getting something she wanted out of the Dotti relationship. A proud and strong-willed

WITH DR DOTTI OUTSIDE HIS HOME IN ROME, 1971

woman, whatever the impression she gave to the press, she would not have put up with his apparent philandering had there not been a very good reason to stay. Perhaps the reason was Luca: perhaps it was just her realization that she no longer had any other role to play in life or on screen, and had better make the most of this one.

Sure there were still offers coming in, by the month if not the week: *Nicholas and Alexandra* for one, *Forty Carats* for another. But neither script (one went to Janet Suzman, the other to Liv Ullmann) really appealed enough to make her break her self-imposed Roman and Swiss exile, and it needs always to be remembered that Audrey was not the kind of actress who really had to act: showbusiness was nowhere near her soul, nor was there ever any particular desire to get back to the cameras and the arc lights. If there was a really good reason to make a film, then she would indeed do so to the best of her considerable ability; but she was never one of those who had to act to live.

And so it was that for all of nine years she stayed away from the screen, until finally they sent her a script she couldn't resist. On the face of it, *Robin and Marian* may have seemed a curious vehicle for a comeback: subtitled 'The Death of Robin Hood', and written by James Goldman who had just triumphed with *The Lion in Winter* which also told of two over-the-hill giants, this was the story of Marian's reunion with Robin twenty years after Sherwood Forest, when he is no longer the merry men's leading brigand but a weary hero back from the Crusades and she has become Abbess of Kirkly.

But something here meant a lot to Audrey, and it was I think the idea of the Abbess as a woman who has given it all up, the romance of the outside world, for a very much more cloistered life and then finds twenty years on that she can no longer bear the isolation and must return to Robin and the real world, however unsatis-

B ACK TO THE MOVIES AFTER AN EIGHT-YEAR ABSENCE TO PLAY THE AGEING MAID
MARIAN OPPOSITE SEAN CONNERY'S EQUALLY AGEING ROBIN HOOD IN *ROBIN AND
MARIAN* (1976): 'WE ARE REMINDED OF HOW LONG IT HAS BEEN SINCE AN ACTRESS
SO BEGUILED US AND CAPTURED OUR IMAGINATION' *TIME*

O N STAGE AT THE OSCARS IN 1976

factory they may turn out to be. This, surely, rang a few bells in her own private life and the director of the film, Dick Lester, surrounded her with the best: Sean Connery as the grizzled, ageing Robin, and a supporting cast led by Robert Shaw, Nicol Williamson, Denholm Elliott and Kenneth Haigh.

'But even with a lovely script and fine actors and a wonderful director,' she told the *International Herald Tribune* on the Pamplona location, 'I still find it terrifying to start a film: I think basically I'm an introvert, and it has always been hard for me to do things in front of people.' Indeed she hadn't even given so much as an interview in the years that she had been away from films, though now she was back she was beginning at last to talk about herself with some kind of spontaneity and insight: 'Filming isn't like riding a bicycle,' she went on, 'it doesn't just come back overnight after so long: even in the best artistic surroundings, in the end you are still alone. Comeback is such a big word, and I'm not sure if I'll stay back: the three men in my life [her husband and two sons] are very different in their ages and their needs and their interests, and someone has to be there, available and adaptable to their programmes, and that someone, I'm happy to say, is me.'

In fact the Dotti marriage was already in severe if not terminal trouble, but as usual Audrey would be the last to explain that to any journalists. She still looked, as one observer noted, like the last woman ever to wear a hat in motion pictures: 'there are people out there who believe that Audrey Hepburn does not perspire, hiccup or sneeze.' But as Hepburn herself was aware, that perception of perfection had led her up a blind alley: a chic façade had somehow been frozen by repetition into empty perfection, and the whole point of *Robin and Marian* was to see whether she could now age into an altogether different kind of actress.

Mad About The Boy

The answer was mixed: critics welcomed her back to the screen, but audiences were less than delighted to find her in sack-cloth and ashes instead of Givenchy or Balmain, and the film did less well than expected at the box-offices of the world. Yet the love affair with Audrey continued: *Time* magazine, the first to put her on its cover back in 1953, was writing twenty-three years later:

'The moment she appears on the screen is startling, not for her thorough, gentle command nor yet for her beauty, which seems heightened and renewed. It is rather that we are reminded of how long it has been since an actress has so beguiled us and captured our imagination. Hepburn is unique, and now almost alone.'

And not only in her professional life: Dotti had made it clear that he would have no other home than Rome, and Audrey was again spending more and more of her time at La Paisible, her beloved Swiss chalet. Not only because the marriage was cracking apart: she had developed a genuine fear and dislike of Rome, one which was heightened when Dotti was involved in an attempted kidnapping outside his hospital. She felt that Sean and Luca, her cherished and idolized children, were no longer safe on the streets of Rome and so Switzerland was once again to be her only real home, a decision which again encouraged Dotti to go his own amorous ways.

Meantime Audrey flew back to Hollywood for a royal return: first she went to appear in a television tribute to William Wyler, then to open *Robin and Marian* at an emotional première: 'Welcome back,' said Jack Valenti, President of the Motion Picture Association of America, 'you've been away too long.'

That too was the feeling shared by the six thousand fans who lined Audrey's route to the Radio City Music Hall when the picture opened in New York: another royal home-coming, well enough intended, but to Audrey a sharp reminder of how much she hated

THE END OF THE SECOND MARRIAGE: 'YOU HOPE THAT IF YOU LOVE SOMEONE, EVERYTHING WILL BE ALL RIGHT,' SHE SAID, 'BUT SOMETIMES IT JUST ISN'T SO' (1979)

Mad About The Boy

public appearances. As soon as she could, she took the plane back to the peace of La Paisible. Other offers came along, easily turned down, though she admitted there was one which got away: nobody ever thought of offering her the Anne Bancroft role in *The Turning Point*, the film about an ageing ballerina which she would have loved to play and for which her background in ballet seemed ideal. 'Mia Farrow gets offered my roles nowadays,' said Audrey at this time, with a rare hint of irony, 'and she's very welcome to most of them.' Three more years elapsed before she went to work again, years in which she tried, for the sake of the children as much as herself, to keep the Dotti marriage alive against increasingly impossible geographic and romantic odds. When she did get back to filming, it was for Terence Young, her director on *Wait Until Dark*, who gave a succinct account of what it took to get Audrey to work:

'First of all you spend a year or so convincing her to accept even the principle that she might make another movie in her life. Then you have to persuade her to read a script. Then you have to make her understand that it is a good script. Then you have to persuade her that she will not be totally destroying her son's life by spending six or eight weeks on a film set. After that, if you are really lucky, she might start talking about the costumes. More probably she'll just say she has to get back to her family and cooking the pasta for dinner, but thank you for thinking of her.'

On this occasion she did consent to a new assignment: quite why she chose *Bloodline*, a Sidney Sheldon thriller of no discernible movie merit, is unclear unless, tiring of the Dotti marriage, she had decided to reassert her independence: by the time the shooting was complete, a divorce was on the cards. Yet on the set she was still the archetypal Audrey: a second marriage in ruins, a difficult thriller to shoot, but time still to reflect to Rex Reed on her good fortune:

Mad About The Boy

'This is by far the happiest time in my life, even with all the unhappiness in the world around me: I'm much less restless now, and no longer searching for the wrong values . . . . I've had so much more than I ever dreamed possible out of life. It's not as though I've had great disappointments, or hopes that didn't work out: I didn't expect anything very much and because of that I'm the least bitter woman I know. I decided years ago to take life unconditionally, and I never expected it to do anything special for me. Yet I've accomplished far more than I ever hoped to, and most of the time it happened without my ever seeking it. I've never even thought of myself as very glamorous: glamorous is Ava Gardner or Elizabeth Taylor, not me. All I really want now is not to be lonely, and to have my garden: I'm glad to have missed what's been happening in the movies these last eight years. It's all been sex and violence, and I'm far too scrawny to strip and I hate guns, so I'm better off out of it.'

She was getting seven hundred and fifty thousand dollars for eight weeks in a Munich studio, co-starring with Ben Gazzara, Omar Sharif, James Mason, Romy Schneider and Irene Papas in a high-class schlock-shocker which did none of those involved any lasting harm, but not a lot of good either: the one truly shocking thing about *Bloodline* was the fact that Audrey only took on her role after it had been turned down by Jacqueline Bisset. During the shooting, she talked to a *Sunday Telegraph* journalist about Ingmar Bergman's *Autumn Sonata* with Ingrid Bergman and Liv Ullmann, and how both actresses had moved her to tears: unspoken here was a sense of her own career path having run abruptly into a dead end. When there were films like that to be made, what the hell was she doing in *Bloodline*?

NEAR HER HOME IN SWITZERLAND, 1979

·158·

Chapter Thirteen

TOWARDS A HAPPY ENDING

66

It's important that I convince Audrey that love is still possible, because I think she must have begun to feel that it's not on the cards for her any more.

ROB WOLDERS

99

By the time Audrey had finished the *Bloodline* shooting, there was a new man in her life, and he was Ben Gazzara. Like her, he was at the end of a marriage (to Janice Rule) and it was largely because of him that she agreed to make her next picture, since he would also be its star. This was to be *They All Laughed*, a curiously unhappy Peter Bogdanovich romantic drama about the estranged wife of a European tycoon who goes to New York in search of love

---

ON LOCATION WITH A NEW LOVE, BEN GAZZARA, FOR SIDNEY SHELDON'S *BLOODLINE* (1979): 'FOR THE LOCATION FILMING IN SICILY,' SAID ONE OF THE CAST, 'AUDREY HAD SEVERAL BODYGUARDS, UNTIL SHE REALIZED THAT EVEN KIDNAP BY THE MAFIA WOULD BE PREFERABLE TO HAVING TO FINISH THIS SCRIPT'

Towards A Happy Ending

and laughter. Written by Bogdanovich himself, in the style of some of Audrey's earlier hits, it was a painful reminder that times had changed, movies had moved on, and *Roman Holiday*s were no longer available for the asking or the echoing.

Nor was the filming in 1980 much helped by a series of disastrous behind-the-camera romantic entanglements: Gazzara went off with a model, Audrey switched her affections to Bogdanovich who in his turn got tragically entangled with a small-part player in the film, Dorothy Stratten, who was murdered by her jealous lover four weeks after the shooting of the picture ended. All in all it was not a happy one, and critical reaction was at best muted, at worst hostile. Audrey Hepburn was only ever to make one more film, and that virtually a guest appearance for Steven Spielberg ten years later. Her love affair with the movies was well and truly over, just three decades after it had started with *Roman Holiday*.

But in her private life, things were looking up: with the divorce from Dotti now in the hands of the lawyers, she was introduced at a dinner party in New York to a young fellow-countryman, Rob Wolders, who had spent many of his recent years looking after a not dissimilar although of course much older actress, Merle Oberon, up to the time of her death. Wolders was, indeed is, a man of tact and discretion who has spent most of his adult life loving and cherishing two older women with a kind of understated brilliance. He had himself briefly been an actor, indeed was involved with Merle in a catastrophic vanity picture called *Interval* at her insistence, but found his true role in support of both Oberon and Hepburn, offering first one and then the other a happiness

WITH SEAN AT THE 1980 AMERICAN FILM INSTITUTE SALUTE TO FRED ASTAIRE

Towards A Happy Ending

they had never found in the company of more dominant or self-centred partners.

So for the last decade of her life, although ironically they never got around to marriage, Audrey at last had her perfect husband: he was independently wealthy from the legacy of Merle Oberon, she had kept much of her movie money, and both were able to live with her sons in Switzerland without needing to work or indeed do anything they had not chosen for themselves.

It was, at last, an idyllic life: Wolders was faithful where Dotti had found that impossible, and he had none of Ferrer's desire to see Audrey maintaining a career. He was just perfect for her, and took considerable pride in sustaining her passion for privacy. They travelled a little, read a lot, cooked for each other, entertained old and discreet friends of the kind who would never reveal the details of their hospitality to the outside world.

No longer subject to the depressions which had always been a part of her earlier marriages, Audrey in her fifties was the perfect homebody wife and mother she had always longed to be: if the movies showed signs of no longer needing her then so be it, she certainly no longer had any need of them. If there were signs that her beloved boys were growing up and away then she still had Wolders, and the Swiss chalet, and a life that could be classed as ideal given the decay and decline into which the careers of many of her generation of stars were now falling. Audrey, as usual, was above and beyond the politics of Hollywood or the Californian search for perpetual youth and novelty; she would grow old gracefully amid the

WITH HER LAST AND GREATEST LOVE, ROBERT WOLDERS,

AT THE 1986 LONDON FILM FESTIVAL

Towards A Happy Ending

Alps, occasionally emerging to remind the rest of the screen world what it was now missing, and what stars once were like. She was her own myth and her own reality: the little-girl-lost who had grown up to be Sabrina Fair and then refused, like the Peter Pan she never got around to filming, to grow old or to make any of the career compromises with age and declining fame which were forced on her less fortunate or happy contemporaries.

Occasionally, journalists would ask why she and Wolders never married: 'We're happy as we are,' said Audrey simply. Wolders once, uncharacteristically, went rather further: 'It wouldn't be fair to suggest something like that to someone who has already gone through two very unhappy marriages. Everyone knows how unhappy her marriage to Mel was, and the second, to Andrea, was even worse. It would be like asking someone who has just got out of an electric chair to sit back on it again.' What her two husbands thought of that comparison is mercifully not on the record. Professionally, in the 1980s, Audrey did very little: from time to time she would make royal returns to Hollywood, no longer to work but to take gracious part in yet another American Film Institute salute to a legendary old star or director with whom she had started out in the 1950s. But then, like some startled gazelle, she would flee back to Switzerland before anyone could start asking too many questions about her private life or her plans for the future.

From time to time she would take odd, lucrative engagements, like a fashion commercial for Japanese television or a 1987 US TV drama with Robert Wagner (*Love Among Thieves*) in which they des-

And with the most faithful of her designers
on screen and off, Givenchy

perately tried to recreate a high-class caper comedy from the 1950s and failed. Then again, she would turn out for Givenchy whenever the old master was having a fashion-house gala, and in 1985 she returned to London to take part in a fund-raiser for the Ballet Rambert which had given her a start on stage almost forty years earlier.

But then, in March 1988, her life changed for the last time: in Tokyo, attending a gala in aid of Unicef, the United Nations Children's Fund, she was asked by its then director James Grant if she would be willing to do something more than turn up (as she had) at the occasional fund-raiser. Such as? Might she be willing to take on the role of its Special Ambassador, one virtually created by Danny Kaye and held since then by both Peter Ustinov and Harry Belafonte? It did not take her long to agree: she of all of them had most cause to be grateful to relief organizations, since her family's lives had been saved by one in Arnhem at the end of the war. Within six weeks she was in Addis Ababa, and for the next three and a half years, until her health began to fail, Audrey was to be found not only in Ethiopia but wherever famine, drought and starvation had created an urgent need for world attention and public money: 'She is no chicken,' wrote Angela Neustatter, 'nudging pensionable age, and she has been in some sort of self-imposed eclipse from stardom for a quarter of a century. But that familiar elfin face is suddenly all over the media again, this time with the reminder that Africa's hunger has not gone away and nor has its need for our charity.'

Audrey now crossed and recrossed America on chat shows with that reminder, and even appeared before Congress committees

---

'SHE NEVER HAD ANY IDEA HOW BEAUTIFUL SHE WAS: AUDREY INVENTED CHIC'

RICHARD AVEDON

Towards A Happy Ending

urging them successfully to boost their aid: 'I went to Ethiopia,' she told Congressmen, 'with so many people telling me how dreadful it would be to see the extent of the suffering. Certainly I saw children in an advanced state of malnutrition . . . but I also witnessed how much is being done to help, and how just a small amount of aid can assist in treating the sick, irrigating the land and planting new crops. I came to realize that the problems of Ethiopia are not insurmountable if only the world will give it just a little more.'

And the world did: Audrey's pleas as an Ambassador for Aid were heard and seen all around the globe because of her fame:

'I have been given the privilege,' she said, 'of speaking for children who cannot speak for themselves, and my task is an easy one because children have no political enemies. To save a child is a blessing: to save a million is a God-given opportunity.'

At long, long last, Audrey had found the 'enormous family' she had always craved; she had also learned that she at last had something of some significance to say to the press: 'We have to give the people of Ethiopia a spade, but then we have to ensure it is used to dig a well instead of yet more graves for dying children.'

Using her face, her fame and her fortune in the service of Unicef's quest for a twelve-million-pound irrigation and reservoir programme, Audrey made her priorities clear:

'If people are still interested in me, if my name makes them listen to what I want to say, then that's wonderful: but I'm not interested in promoting Audrey Hepburn or another movie these days. I want to tell the world how it can help Ethiopia, and why I still feel

---

THE LAST FILM: *ALWAYS* (1990): 'OH GOD, HOW WE ARE GOING TO MISS HER', STEVEN SPIELBERG, FOR WHOM SHE PLAYED THE ANGEL

Towards A Happy Ending

optimistic despite all the harrowing and dreadful things I saw there. A thousand children a day are still dying of malnutrition and illness, but so much is now being done that I know things will get better.'

At the end of 1989 she took time off from her role as Unicef Ambassador to make one last film, Steven Spielberg's *Always*, in which she played the guardian angel in a long, white turtleneck sweater who welcomes the newly-dead hero Richard Dreyfuss to the afterlife. It was not the most successful or wonderful of farewell movies, but as Philip French concluded for the *Observer*: 'The main consolation this picture offers is that our first close encounter after death will be with an angelic Audrey Hepburn at her most radiant. Dante himself never made heaven look so inviting.'

But then it was back on the road for Unicef, back to the Sudan and Ethiopia, and by now everything she did was in their name and for their benefit, even the heart-breaking recital of *Anne Frank's Diary* which she read to the orchestral backing of Michael Tilson Thomas and the LSO at the Barbican in May 1991:

'An actress is not something I ever really became,' she told Lesley Garner for the *Sunday Telegraph* at that time, 'and I act the same way now as I did forty years ago: I was never backed up by a professional training, had no Shakespeare at school, none of that. I had to skip it all and do it with feeling instead of technique . . . all my life I've been in situations where I've had no technique, but if you feel enough you can get away with murder.'

In a sense, Audrey never really retired or retreated; there was no separation between the public and the private, just a sense that

THE WAY WE WERE: WITH HER FIRST CO-STAR, GREGORY PECK,

AT A VENICE TRIBUTE TO INGRID BERGMAN

Towards A Happy Ending

now it had all come together. She had found the role she was born to play, as a children's ambassador to the world at large, and it required no acting at all.

A month or so before her Barbican stage appearance, the first she had made in London in forty years and also alas the last, she had been honoured with a retrospective at Lincoln Center in New York, where her surviving directors Billy Wilder and Stanley Donen and such co-stars as Gregory Peck, Alan Arkin and Tony Perkins all gathered to do her homage. But there was a sense now that the movies were already a thing of her past, and that she had found a world elsewhere. As Harry Belafonte told that fashionable Manhattan movie audience, 'You have not seen the real Audrey until you have seen her in the jungles of Bangladesh, in Thailand, in Vietnam, in the holding camps of the dispossessed world among hundreds of starving people.'

For the past three years, and into what were now to be the last two of her life, Audrey had toured not just Africa but Bangladesh, Thailand, Guatemala, Mexico, El Salvador, Honduras and Venezuela as a goodwill ambassador: 'The human obligation,' she said in 1992, 'is to help children who are suffering anywhere in the world. All the rest is luxury and trivial. But there's no way I could have done any of this without Robbie: he's the one who gets the flights and the hotels for free when Unicef can't afford to send me on their budget. He's the one who checks the mikes in the hotel rooms before the press conferences, and he's the one who encouraged me to make it a full-time occupation. We found each other at a

'I HAVE SEEN FAMINE IN ETHIOPIA AND BANGLADESH, BUT I HAVE SEEN NOTHING LIKE THIS' AUDREY IN SOMALIA FOR UNICEF, A FEW MONTHS BEFORE SHE DIED

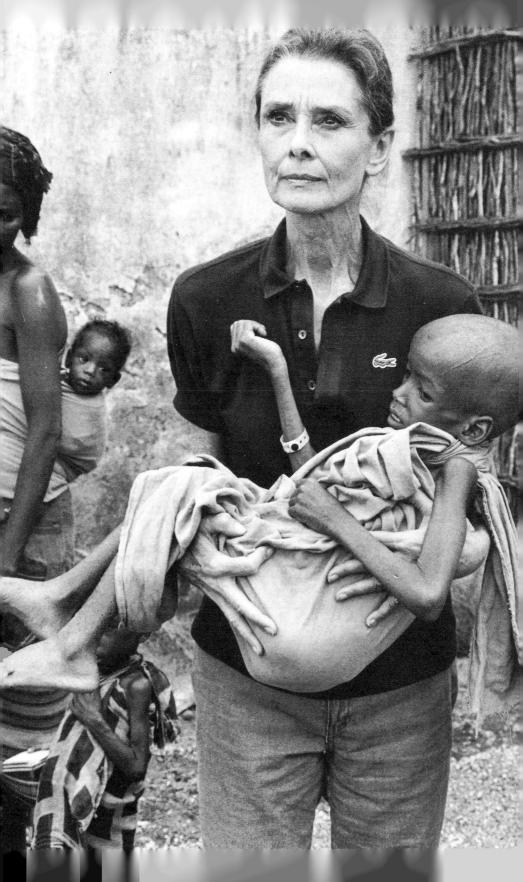

Towards A Happy Ending

time in our lives when we were both terribly unhappy, and yet we've been able to make each other very happy ever since. You can't ask for more than that, now can you?'

But now, in late 1992, there was something else: Audrey began looking, even by her standards, desperately emaciated and exhausted. The face once described by Cecil Beaton as 'a Modigliani on which the paint has hardly dried,' suddenly began to look hollow and desperately care-worn and older, much older, than its sixty-two years. At first, nobody wanted to believe what should have been staring at us in that face: 'She's tired,' we said. 'Ethiopia,' we said. 'The strain of all that travelling: besides, she's always been painfully thin.'

And then suddenly she was in Los Angeles, at the Cedars Sinai Medical Center where they confirmed, on 12 November 1992, what American supermarket tabloids had been screeching for a week: 'Hepburn has cancer.' It was as simple as that: a colon tumour was removed, but it was already too late. Givenchy sent his private Gulfstream jet to bring her home to Switzerland for Christmas and what she now knew were the last few weeks of her life. Old friends gathered round, notably Roger Moore whom she asked to succeed her as the Unicef Special Ambassador, but so far as possible her privacy was maintained to the last. The Swiss are good at that: villagers joined with her sons and Robbie Wolders in fending off the eyes of an outside world, and when on 20 January she died it was as she had so wished, in her own bed at La Paisible surrounded by Robbie and her sons. The other two men in her life, Mel Ferrer and Andrea Dotti, arrived for the funeral a few days later, both looking as shell-

---

'A CHILD IS A CHILD IN ANY COUNTRY,

NO MATTER THE POLITICS'

Towards A Happy Ending

shocked as if they had still been married to her, and their sense of loss was echoed from the church bells of that small Swiss village around the world:

'This gamine turned legend,' wrote Martha Sherrill for the *International Herald Tribune*, 'transcended all the fads and the phoniness of her profession . . . She transcended gloom and everydayness with a rare combination of fragility and abandon and ancient European wisdom . . . . She never seemed to be trying, or wanting: she just existed, but you know? That was enough.'

At the small, family funeral in Tolochenaz, someone said that at last Audrey had found 'the room somewhere, far away from the cold night air' that Eliza sang about in *My Fair Lady*: but in reality that room was the world, and her family, the one she had always wanted, was the world-wide family of Unicef. It was left to another of its ambassadors, Sir Peter Ustinov, to write the best of her many obituaries:

'Statistics tell us that Audrey died young: what no statistics can show is that Audrey would have died young at any age. With the perfect bone structure of her face, she seemed to possess the secret of a youth verging on the eternal, and yet the poise of maturity was already with her from a very early age. There is no doubt that the actual contact with starving children affected her very deeply, but

'NOTHING, NO NEWSPAPER OR TELEVISION REPORTING, COULD HAVE PREPARED ME FOR THE UNSPEAKABLE AGONY I FELT SEEING COUNTLESS LITTLE, FRAGILE, EMACIATED CHILDREN SITTING UNDER THE TREES WAITING TO BE FED, MOST OF THEM TERRIBLY ILL. I SHALL NEVER FORGET THEIR HUGE EYES IN TINY FACES, AND THE TERRIBLE SILENCE.' AUDREY WON A POSTHUMOUS OSCAR IN 1993 IN RECOGNITION OF HER WORK FOR UNICEF IN AFRICA AND AROUND THE WORLD

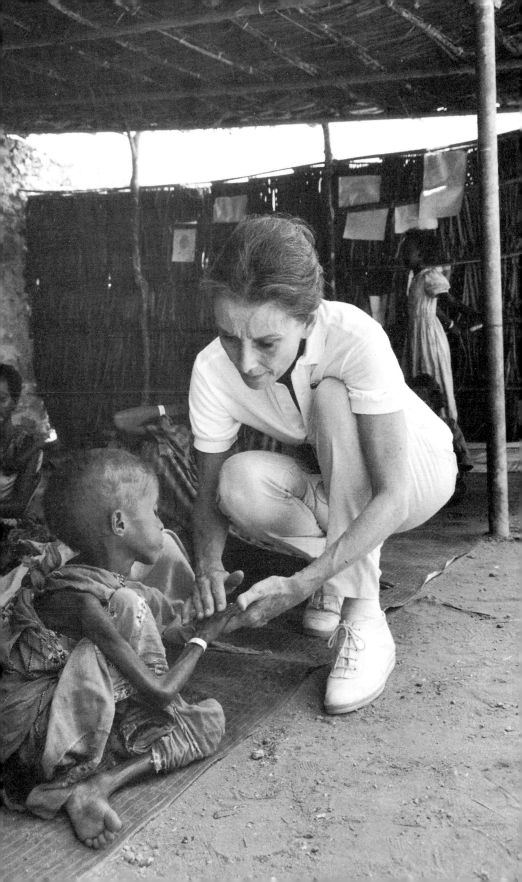

Towards A Happy Ending

there was nothing overtly emotional about her ability to stoke up the embers of the public conscience. Nothing was needed other than the evidence itself, and the restrained eloquence which she displayed on every occasion. There was never anyone further away from the conventional image of showbusiness glitz and glamour. Nature had given her all the mystery she needed, and although her words were selected with the care of a poet, they only served to emphasize the fact that they were not merely at the service of a fine mind, but also the instruments of a tender and yet steadfast heart. Audrey made a magnificent contribution to her art, and she died some way beyond the line of duty. We sense her loss as a friend, as an acquaintance and as a personality. As an example, and therefore as a human being, she is still very much alive.'

Audrey Hepburn, 1929–1993: a tender and steadfast heart. We shall not see her like again, except, thank God, on the films she left us to remember her by, and in the memories of those who were visited, or appealed to, by the greatest of goodwill ambassadors.

AUDREY HEPBURN, 1929-1993: 'REMEMBER,' SHE WROTE IN A FAREWELL LETTER TO HER TWO SONS, 'IF YOU EVER NEED A HELPING HAND, IT'S AT THE END OF YOUR ARM. AS YOU GET OLDER, REMEMBER YOU HAVE ANOTHER HAND: THE FIRST IS TO HELP YOURSELF, THE SECOND IS TO HELP OTHERS.' IN THE FACES OF THE CHILDREN OF SOMALIA,' SAID THE PASTOR AT HER FUNERAL IN JANUARY 1993, 'WAS REFLECTED THE LIGHT OF HER SMILE.'

Chapter Fourteen

FILMOGRAPHY

1 LAUGHTER IN PARADISE. Great Britain. Associated British Pictures, 1951. Produced and directed by Mario Zampi. Written by Michael Pertwee and Jack Davies. Photographed by William McLeod. Music by Stanley Black. Edited by Giulio Zampi. Art Direction by Ivan King. With Alastair Sim, Fay Compton, Beatrice Campbell, Veronica Hurst, Guy Middleton, A. E. Matthews, Joyce Grenfell, Anthony Steel, John Laurie, Eleanor Summerfield, Ronald Adam, Leslie Dwyer, Ernest Thesiger, Hugh Griffith, Michael Pertwee, Audrey Hepburn (*Cigarette Girl*), Mackenzie Ward, Charlotte Mitchell, Colin Gordon, Mary Germaine, Noel Howlett, Martin Boddey.

2 THE LAVENDER HILL MOB. Great Britain. Ealing Studios, 1951. Produced by Michael Balcon. Directed by Charles Crichton. Written by T. E. B. Clarke. Photographed by Douglas Slocombe. Music by Georges Auric. Edited by Seth Holt. Musical Direction by Ernest Irving. Art Direction by William Kellner. With Alec Guinness, Stanley Holloway, Sidney James, Alfie Bass, Marjorie Fielding, John Gregson, Edie Martin, Clive Morton, Ronald Adam, Sydney Tafler, Jacques Brunius, Meredith Edwards, Gibb McLaughlin, Patrick Barr, Marie Burke, Audrey Hepburn (*Chiquita*), John Salew, Arthur Hambling, Frederick Piper, Peter Bull, Patric Doonan, Alanna Boyce, William Fox, Michael Trubshawe, Ann Heffernan, Eugene Deckers, Paul Demel, Andrea Malandrinos, Cyril Chamberlain, Tony Quinn, Moutrie Kelsall, Christopher Hewitt, David Davies, Joe Clarke, Charles Lamb, Archie Duncan, Fred Griffiths, Frank Forsyth, Arthur Mullard, Jacques Cey, Marie Ney, John Warwick, Robert Shaw.

3 YOUNG WIVES' TALE. Great Britain. Associated British Pictures, 1951. Produced by Victor Skutetzky. Directed by Henry Cass. Written by Ann Burnaby, from the play by Ronald Jeans. Photographed by Erwin Hillier. Music by Philip Green. Edited by E. Jarvis. Music Direction by Louis Levy. Art Direction by Terence Verity. With Joan Greenwood, Nigel Patrick, Derek Farr, Guy Middleton, Athene Seyler, Helen Cherry, Audrey Hepburn (*Eve Lester*), Fabia Drake, Irene Handl, Joan Sanderson, Selma Vaz Dias, Jack McNaughton, Brian Oulton, Carol James.

4 THE SECRET PEOPLE. Great Britain. Ealing Studios, 1952. Produced by Sidney Cole. Directed by Thorold Dickinson. Written by Thorold Dickinson, Wolfgang Wilhelm and Christianna Brand, from a story by Thorold Dickinson and Joyce Carey. Photographed by Gordon Dines. Music by Roberto Gerhard. Edited by Peter Tanner. Art Direction by William Kellner. Costumes by Anthony Mendleson. Choreography by Andree Howard. With Valentina Cortesa, Serge Reggiani, Charles Goldner, Audrey Hepburn (*Nora Brentano*), Angeles Fouldes, Megs Jenkins, Irene Worth, Reginald Tate, Norman Williams, Michael Shepley, Athene Seyler, Sydney Tafler, Geoffrey Hibbert, John Ruddock, Michael Allan, John Field, Bob Monkhouse, Hugo Schuster, Charlie Cairoli & Paul, Lionel Harris, Rollo Gamble, John Penrose, John Chandos, Michael Ripper, Yvonne Coulette, John Mansi, John Gabriel, Olga Landiak, Frederick Schiller, Phaedros Antonio, Gaston Richer, Derek Elphinstone, Edward Evans, Ingeborg Wells, Helen Ford, Ann Lancaster, Grace Draper, Bertram Shuttleworth, Pamela Harrington, John Allen, Joe Linnane, Bay White, Sam Kydd, Simone Silva.

5 MONTE CARLO BABY (NOUS IRONS A MONTE CARLO). France. GFD/Favorite Pictures, 1952. Produced by Ray Ventura. Directed by Jean Boyer and Lester Fuller. Written by Jean Boyer, Lester Fuller, and Alex Joffe. Photographed by Charles Suin. Music by Paul Misraki. Edited by Franchette Mazin. Art Direction by Robert Giordani. Music and lyrics by Paul Misraki and Geoffrey Parsons. With Audrey Hepburn (*Linda Farrel*), Jules Munshin, Michele Farmer, Cara Williams, Philippe Lemaire, Russell Collins, Ray Ventura and His Orchestra.

6 ROMAN HOLIDAY. Paramount, 1953. Produced and directed by William Wyler. Written by Ian McLellan Hunter and John Dighton, from a story by Ian McLellan Hunter. Photographed by Frank F. Planer and Henri Alekan. Music by Georges Auric. Edited by Robert Swink. Art Direction by Hal Pereira and Walter Tyler. Costumes by Edith Head. With Gregory Peck, Audrey Hepburn (*Princess Anne*), Eddie Albert, Hartley Power, Laura Solari, Harcourt Williams, Margaret Rawlings, Tullio Carminati, Paolo Carlini, Claudio Ermelli, Paolo Borboni, Heinz Hindrich, Gorella Gori, Alfredo Rizzo, John Horne, Count Andre Eszterhazy, Col. Ugo Ballerini, Ugo De Pascale, Bruno Baschiera, Princess Alma Cattaneo, Diane Lante, Giacomo Penza, Eric Oulton, Rapindranath Mitter, Princess Lilamani, Cesare Viori, Col. Nichola Kohopleff, Baroness Teresa Gauthier, Hari Singh, Kmark Singh, Luigi Bocchi, Helen Fondra, Mario Lucinni,

Gherdo Fehrer, Luis Marino, Armando Annuale, Luigi Moneta, Marco Tulli, Maurizio Arena, John Fostini, George Higgins, Alfred Browne, John Cortay, Richard McNamara.

7 SABRINA FAIR. Paramount, 1954. Produced and directed by Billy Wilder. Written by Billy Wilder, Samuel Taylor, and Ernest Lehman, from the play *Sabrina Fair* by Samuel Taylor. Photographed by Charles Lang, Jr. Music by Frederick Hollander. Edited by Arthur Schmidt. Art Direction by Hal Pereira and Walter Tyler. Costumes by Edith Head. Music and lyrics by Wilson Stone, Richard Rodgers, Lorenz Hart, Harold Lewis, Louiguy, Edith Piaf, Frank Silver, Irving Cohen, and John Cope. With Humphrey Bogart, Audrey Hepburn (*Sabrina Fairchild*), William Holden, Walter Hampden, John Williams, Martha Hyer, Joan Vohs, Marcel Dalio, Marcel Hillaire, Nella Walker, Francis X. Bushman, Ellen Corby, Marjorie Bennett, Emory Parnell, Kay Riehl, Nancy Kulp, Kay Kuter, Paul Harvey, Emmett Vogan, Colin Campbell, Harvey Dunn, Marion Ross, Charles Harvey, Greg Stafford, Bill Neff, Otto Forrest, David Ahdar, Rand Harper.

8 WAR AND PEACE. Italy/USA. Ponti-De Laurentiis Productions/Paramount, 1956. Produced by Dino De Laurentiis. Directed by King Vidor. Written by Bridget Boland, Robert Westerby, King Vidor, Mario Camerini, Ennio De Concini, Ivo Perilli, and Irwin Shaw, from the novel by Leo Tolstoy. Photographed by Jack Cardiff and Aldo Tonti. Music by Nino Rota. Edited by Stuart Gilmore and Leo Cattozzo. Music Direction by Franco Ferrera. Art Direction by Mario Chiari, Franz Bachelin, and Giani Polidori. Costumes by Maria De Matteis. With Audrey Hepburn (*Natasha Rostov*), Henry Fonda, Mel Ferrer, Vittorio Gassman, John Mills, Herbert Lom, Oscar Homolka, Anita Ekberg, Helmut Dantine, Barry Jones, Anna Maria Ferrero, Milly Vitale, Jeremy Brett, Lea Seidl, Wilfrid Lawson, Sean Barrett, Tullio Carminati, May Britt, Patrick Crean, Gertrude Flynn, Teresa Pellati, Maria Zanoli, Alberto Carlo Lolli, Mario Addobati, Gualtiero Tumiati, Clelia Matania, Gianni Luda, Eschilo Tarquini, Alex D'Alessio, Alfred Rizzo, Mauro Lanciani, Ina Alexeiva, Don Little, John Horne.

9 FUNNY FACE. Paramount, 1957. Produced by Roger Edens. Directed by Stanley Donen. Written by Leonard Gershe, from his musical libretto, *Wedding Day*. Photographed by Ray June. Music by George Gershwin, Ira Gershwin,

Roger Edens and Leonard Gershe. Edited by Frank Bracht. Musical Direction by Adolph Deutsch. Art Direction by George W. Davis and Hal Pereira. Costumes by Edith Head and Hubert de Givenchy. Choreography by Fred Astaire and Eugene Loring. With Audrey Hepburn (*Jo Stockton*), Fred Astaire, Kay Thompson, Michel Auclair, Robert Fleming, Dovima, Virginia Gibson, Suzy Parker, Sunny Harnett, Don Powell, Carole Eastman, Sue England, Ruta Lee, Alex Gerry, Iphigenie Castiglioni, Jean Del Val, Albert D'Arno, Nina Borget, Marilyn White, Dorothy Colbert, Louise Glenn, Heather Hopper, Cecile Rogers, Nancy Kilgas, Emilie Stevens, Paul Smith, Diane Du Bois, Karen Scott, Gabriel Curtiz, Peter Camlin, Elizabeth Slifer, Donald Lawton, Karine Nordman, Genevieve Aumont, Nesdon Booth, George Dee, Marcel de la Brosse, Albert Goddiris, Jerry Lucas, Jack Chefe, Jan Bradley.

10 LOVE IN THE AFTERNOON. Allied Artists, 1957. Produced and directed by Billy Wilder. Written by Billy Wilder and I. A. L. Diamond, from the novel *Ariane* by Claude Anet. Photographed by William Mellor. Music by Franz Waxman. Edited by Leonid Azar. Art Direction by Alexander Trauner. Costumes by Hubert de Givenchy. With Gary Cooper, Audrey Hepburn (*Ariane Chavasse*), Maurice Chevalier, Van Doude, John McGiver, Lise Bourdin, Bonifas, Audrey Wilder, Gyula Kokas, Michel Kokas, George Cocos, Victor Gazzoli, Olga Valery, Leila Croft, Valerie Croft, Charles Bouillard, Minerva Pious, Filo, Andre Priez, Gaidon, Gregory Gromoff, Janine Dard, Claude Ariel, Francois Moustache, Gloria France, Jean Sylvain, Annie Roudier, Jeanne Charblay, Odette Charblay, Gilbert Constant, Monique Saintey, Jacques Preboist, Anne Laurent, Jacques Ary, Simone Vanlancker, Richard Flagy, Jeanne Papir, Marcelle Broc, Marcelle Praince, Guy Delorme, Olivia Chevalier, Solon Smith, Eve Marley, Jean Rieubon, Christian Lude, Charles Lemontier, Emile Mulor, Alexander Trauner, Betty Schneider

11 THE NUN'S STORY. Warner Brothers, 1959. Produced by Henry Blanke. Directed by Fred Zinnemann. Written by Robert Anderson, from the book by Kathryn C. Hulme. Photographed by Franz F. Planer. Music by Franz Waxman. Edited by Walter Thompson. Art Direction by Alexander Trauner. Costumes by Marjorie Best. With Audrey Hepburn (*Sister Luke, Gabrielle Van Der Mal*), Peter Finch, Edith Evans, Peggy Ashcroft, Dean Jagger, Mildred Dunnock, Beatrice Straight, Patricia Collinge, Eva Kotthaus, Ruth White, Niall McGinnis, Patricia Bosworth, Barbara O'Neil, Lionel Jeffries, Margaret

Phillips, Rosalie Crutchley, Colleen Dewhurst, Stephen Murray, Orlando Martins, Errol John, Jeannette Sterke, Richard O'Sullivan, Diana Lambert, Marina Wolkonsky, Penelope Horner, Ave Ninchi, Charles Lamb, Ludovice Bonhomme, Dara Gavin, Elfrida Simarbi, Dorothy Alison, Molly Urquhart, Frank Singuineau, Juan Aymerich, Giovanna Galletti.

12 GREEN MANSIONS. Metro-Goldwyn-Mayer, 1959. Produced by Edmund Grainger. Directed by Mel Ferrer. Written by Dorothy Kingsley, from the novel by William Henry Hudson. Photographed by Joseph Ruttenberg. Music by Hector Villa-Lobos and Bronislau Kaper. Edited by Ferris Webster. Art Direction by William A. Horning and Preston Ames. Costumes by Dorothy Jeakins. Choreography by Katharine Dunham. With Audrey Hepburn (*Rima*), Anthony Perkins, Lee J. Cobb, Sessue Hayakawa, Henry Silva, Nehemiah Persoff, Michael Pate, Estelle Hemsley, Bill Saito, Yoneo Iguchi.

13 THE UNFORGIVEN. Hecht-Hill-Lancaster Productions/United Artists, 1960. Produced by James Hill. Directed by John Huston. Written by Ben Maddow, from the novel by Alan LeMay. Photographed by Franz E. Planer. Music and Music Direction by Dimitri Tiomkin. Edited by Russell Lloyd. Art Direction by Stephen Grimes. With Burt Lancaster, Audrey Hepburn (*Rachel Zachary*), Audie Murphy, John Saxon, Charles Bickford, Lillian Gish, Albert Salmi, Joseph Wiseman, June Walker, Kipp Hamilton, Arnold Merritt, Carlos Rivas, Doug McClure.

14 BREAKFAST AT TIFFANY'S. Paramount, 1961. Produced by Martin Jurow and Richard Shepherd. Directed by Blake Edwards. Written by George Axelrod, from the novella by Truman Capote. Photographed by Franz E. Planer. Music by Henry Mancini. Edited by Howard Smith. Costumes by Edith Head. Music and lyrics of *Moon River* by Henry Mancini and Johnny Mercer. With Audrey Hepburn (*Holly Golightly*), George Peppard, Patricia Neal, Buddy Ebsen, Martin Balsam, Mickey Rooney, Villalonga, John McGiver, Dorothy Whitney, Stanly Adams, Elvia Allman, Alan Reed Sr, Beverly Hills, Claude Stroud, Putney.

15 THE CHILDREN'S HOUR. United Artists, 1961. Produced and directed by William Wyler. Written by John Michael Hayes. Adaptation by Lillian Hellman from her play. Photographed by Franz E. Planer. Music by Alex North. Edited by Robert Swink. Art Direction by Fernando Carrere. Costumes by Dorothy Jeakins. With Audrey Hepburn (*Karen Wright*), Shirley MacLaine, JamesGarner, Miriam Hopkins, Fay Bainter, Karen Balkin, Veronica Cartwright, Jered Barclay, Mimi Gibson, William Mims, Hope Summers, Florence MacMichael.

16 CHARADE. Universal, 1963. Produced and directed by Stanley Donen. Written by Peter Stone, from the story *The Unsuspecting Wife* by Marc Behm and Peter Stone. Photographed by Charles Lang Jr. Music by Henry Mancini. Edited by James Clark. Art Direction by Jean d'Eaubonne. Miss Hepburn's costumes by Hubert de Givenchy. Music and lyrics by Henry Mancini and Johnny Mercer. With Cary Grant, Audrey Hepburn (*Regina Lambert*), Walter Matthau, James Coburn, George Kennedy, Ned Glass, Jacques Marin, Paul Bonifas, Dominique Minot, Thomas Chelimsky.

17 PARIS WHEN IT SIZZLES. Paramount, 1964. Produced by Richard Quine and George Axelrod. Directed by Richard Quine. Written by George Axelrod, from the story by Julien Duvivier and Henri Jeanson. Photographed by Charles Lang, Jr. Music by Nelson Riddle. Edited by Archie Marshek. Art Direction by Jean d'Eaubonne. Costumes by Hubert de Givenchy and Christian Dior. With William Holden, Audrey Hepburn (*Gabrielle Simpson*), Gregoire Aslan, Raymond Bussieres, Christian Duvallex, Noël Coward, Tony Curtis, Marlene Dietrich, Mel Ferrer, Thomas Michel, Dominique Boschero, Evi Marandi, and the singing voices of Fred Astaire and Frank Sinatra.

18 MY FAIR LADY. Warner Brothers, 1964. Produced by Jack L. Warner. Directed by George Cukor. Written by Alan Jay Lerner, from a musical play by Alan Jay Lerner and Frederick Loewe, and the play *Pygmalion* by George Bernard Shaw. Photographed by Harry Stading. Music by Frederick Loewe. Edited by William Ziegler. Production Design by Cecil Beaton. Musical Direction by André Previn. Art Direction by Gene Allen. Costumes by Cecil Beaton. Choreography by Hermes Pan. With Audrey Hepburn (*Eliza Doolittle*), Rex Harrison, Stanley Holloway, Wilfrid Hyde-White, Gladys Cooper, Jeremy Brett, Theodore Bikel, Isobel Elsom, Mona Washbourne, John Alderson, John McLiam, Marni Nixon, Bill Shirley, Ben Wrigley, Clive Halliday, Richard Peel, Eric Heath, James O'Hara, Kendrick Huxham, Frank Baker, Walter Burke, Queenie Leonard, Laurie Main, Maurice Dallimore,

Owen McGiveney, Jack Raine, Marjorie Bennett, Britannia Beatey, Beatrice Greenough, Hilda Plowright, Dinah Anne Rogers, Lois Battle, Jacqueline Squire, Gwen Watts, Eugene Hoffman, Kai Farrelli, Raymond Foster, Joe Evans, Marie Busch, Mary Alexander, William Linkie, Henry Sweetman, Andrew Brown.

19 HOW TO STEAL A MILLION. Twentieth Century-Fox, 1966. Produced by Fred Kohlmar. Directed by William Wyler. Written by Harry Kurnitz, from the story *Venus Rising* by George Bradshaw. Photographed by Charles Lang. Music by Johnny Williams. Edited by Robert Swink. Production Design by Alexander Trauner. Costumes by Hubert de Givenchy. With Audrey Hepburn (*Nicole Bonnet*), Peter O'Toole, Eli Wallach, Hugh Griffith, Charles Boyer, Fernand Gravey, Marcel Dalio, Jacques Marin, Francois Moustache, Roger Treville, Eddie Malin, Bert Bertram, Louise Chevalier, Remy Longa, Gil Delamare.

20 TWO FOR THE ROAD. Twentieth Century-Fox, 1967. Produced and directed by Stanley Donen. Written by Frederic Raphael. Photographed by Christopher Challis. Music by Henry Mancini. Edited by Richard Marden and Madeleine Gug. Art Direction by Willy Holt and Marc Frederic. Costumes by Hardy Amies, Ken Scott, Michele Posier, Paco Rabanne, Mary Quant, Foale and Tuffin. With Audrey Hepburn (*Joanna Wallace*), Albert Finney, Eleanor Bron, William Daniels, Claude Dauphin, Nadia Gray, Georges Descrieres, Gabrielle Middleton, Jacqueline Bisset, Judy Cornwell, Irene Hilda, Dominique Joos, Kathy Chelimsky, Carol Van Dyke, Karyn Balm, Mario Verdon, Roger Dann, Libby Morris, Yves Barsacq, Helene Tossy, Jean-Francois Lalet, Albert Michel, Joanna Jones, Sophia Torkell, Patricia Viterbo, Olga George Picot, Clarissa Hillel, Cathy Jones.

21 WAIT UNTIL DARK. Warner Brothers, 1967. Produced by Mel Ferrer. Directed by Terence Young. Written by Robert Carrington and Jane Howard-Carrington, from the play by Frederick Knott. Photographed by Charles Lang. Music by Henry Mancini. Edited by Gene Milford. Art Direction by George Jenkins. Music and lyrics of *Wait Until Dark* by Henry Mancini, Jay Livingston and Ray Evans, sung by Bobby Darin. With Audrey Hepburn (*Susy Hendrix*), Alan Arkin, Richard Crenna, Efrem Zimbalist Jr, Jack Weston, Samantha Jones, Julie Herrod, Frank O'Brien, Gary Morgan, Jean Del Val.

Filmography

22 <u>ROBIN AND MARIAN</u>. Great Britain. Columbia, 1976. Produced by Denis O'Dell. Directed by Richard Lester. Written by James Goldman. Photographed by David Watkin. Music by John Barry. Edited by John Victor Smith. Production Design by Michael Stringer. Art Direction by Gil Parrando. Costumes by Yvonne Blake. With Sean Connery, Audrey Hepburn (*Maid Marian*), Robert Shaw, Richard Harris, Nicol Williamson, Denholm Elliott, Kenneth Haigh, Ronnie Barker, Ian Holm, Bill Maynard, Esmond Knight, Veronica Quilligan, Peter Butterworth, John Barrett, Kenneth Cranhan, Victoria Merida Roja, Montserrat Julio, Victoria Hernandez Sanguino, Margarita Minguillon.

23 <u>SIDNEY SHELDON'S BLOODLINE</u>. Paramount, 1979. Produced by David V. Picker and Sidney Beckerman. Directed by Terence Young. Written by Laird Koenig, from the novel by Sidney Sheldon. Photographed by Freddie Young. Music by Ennio Morricone. Edited by Bud Molin. Production Design by Ted Haworth. Costumes by Enrico Sabbatini. With Audrey Hepburn (*Elizabeth Roffe*), Ben Gazzara, James Mason, Claudia Mori, Irene Papas, Michelle Phillips, Maurice Ronet, Romy Schneider, Omar Sharif, Beatrice Straight, Gert Frobe, Wolfgang Preiss, Marcel Bozzuffi, Pinkas Braun, Wulf Kessler.

24 <u>THEY ALL LAUGHED</u>. Time-Life Films/Twentieth Century-Fox, 1981. Produced by George Morfogen and Blaine Novak. Directed and written by Peter Bogdanovich. Photographed by Robby Muller. Music by Douglas Dilge. Edited by Scott Vickrey. Art Direction by Kert Lundell. With Audrey Hepburn (*Angela Niotes*), Ben Gazzara, John Ritter, Colleen Camp, Patti Hansen, Dorothy Stratten, George Morfogen, Blaine Novak, Sean Ferrer, Linda MacEwen, Glenn Scarpelli, Vassily Lambrinos, Antonia Bogdanovich, Alexandra Bogdanovich, Sheila Stodden, Lisa Dunsheath, Joyce Hyser, Elizabeth Pena, Riccardo Bertoni, Shawn Casey, Earl Poole Ball, Jo-El Sonnier, Eric Kaz, Ken Kosek, Larry Campbell, Lincoln Schleifer, John Sholle, Brigitte Catapano, Parris Bruckner, Vivien Landau, Lillian Silverstone, Steve Cole, Steven Fromewick, Tzi Ma, William Craft, William DeNino, Kelly Donnally, Linda Ray, Andrea Weber, Spike Spigener, Nick Micskey, Robert Hawes, Michael McGifford, Vittorio Tiburz, Alex MacArthur, George Cardini, Robert Skilling, Kennely Noble, Anthony Paige, Violetta Landek.

Filmography

25 <u>ALWAYS</u>. Universal-United Artists, 1990. Produced by Steven Spielberg, Frank Marshall, and Kathleen Kennedy. Directed by Steven Spielberg. Written by Jerry Belson, from the screenplay *A Guy Names Joe* by Dalton Trumbo, from a story by Frederick Hazlitt Brennan, Chandler Sprague, and David Boehm. Photographed by Mikael Salomon. Edited by Michael Kahn. Music by John Williams. Production Design by James Bissell. Art Direction by Chris Burian-Mohr. Costumes by Ellen Mirojnick. Choreography by Bob Banas. With Richard Dreyfuss, Holly Hunter, Brad Johnson, John Goodman, Audrey Hepburn (*Hap*), Roberts Blossom, Keith David, Ed Van Nuys, Marg Helgenberger, Dale Dye, Brian Haley, James Lashly, Michael Steve Jones, Kim Robillard, Jim Sparkman, Doug McGrath, Joseph McCrossin, J. D. Souther, Gerry Rothschild, Loren Smothers, Taleena Ottwell.

Acknowledgements

BFI Stills, Posters and Design, London.
Hulton Deutsch Collection, London.
The Kobal Collection, London, with acknowledgement to Allied Artists; Associated British; Columbia Pictures; Ealing Studios/Rank; MGM; Paramount; Twentieth-Century Fox; United Artists; Universal International; Universal Pictures; Warner Brothers.
Popperfoto, Northampton.
Rex Features Ltd. London.
David Seymour/Magnum Photos Ltd, London.
Dennis Stock/Magnum Photos Ltd, London.
© 1993 Time Inc., New York. Reprinted by permission.
Unicef/Betty Press.
Unicef/Jeremy Hartley.
Unicef/John Isaac.
© 1993 Bob Willoughby for permission to reproduce his previously unpublished photographs taken on the sets of *The Children's Hour* (1961) p.114, and *My Fair Lady* (1964) p.125-126.
The LUX advertisement was reprinted with permission of the proprietor of the LUX Trade Mark.

Index